HOW TO BUILD SALES CONFIDENCE

BY

JAMES SKI
CEO AND FOUNDER,
SALES CONFIDENCE

ISBN: 979-8-89109-685-1 - paperback
ISBN: 979-8-89109-686-8 - ebook

TABLE OF CONTENTS

Foreword

I met James Ski on a TikTok Live. On this Live I was giving away money to help people fund their dreams. I'm dedicating my life to the pursuit of helping people achieve their dreams.

When James came on I immediately resonated with his mission to help people around the world improve their sales skills and build more confidence in themselves.

In my 30 years of experience building and investing in businesses. The greatest success or failure in any business I have been involved in has been the ability of people in my teams to make sales.

Learning to sell is the single best skill you can learn to be more successful in business or sales.

Right back to that very first conversation with James - I felt his passion for sales and his motivation to help people succeed. So much so I agreed to mentor him for £10k. I have never done this before or since. In fact I later returned his money because I believe in "Giving without taking" and I preferred James to invest this money back into his dream.

I have also been very taken aback by James's story of living with bipolar disorder. He seems to have developed excellent empathy and understanding of people through his experiences giving him a deep emotional understanding of people and their needs. This is what sales is really about - learning how people behave and supporting them with their goals and solving their problems.

James has gone extremely deep in this book on the mindset of what it takes to be successful in sales as a business owner, sales person, coach or entrepreneur. I really appreciate his practical tips on confidence and developing unwavering self belief in what you are selling. Without this you will not succeed.

I'm absolutely honored to have written the foreword to his book "How to build Sales Confidence".

As the Founder of Helpbnk (A global community to help people achieve their dreams with free advice and guidance) and an investor and encourager of people pursuing their dreams. I wish everyone more success by picking up and reading this book. Without sales there's no business.

Simon Squibb
Investor & Founder, HelpBnk
https://helpbnk.com/

What To Expect

The book is divided into three pillars with each focused on a different aspect of building sales confidence.

For example, in the first pillar, Mindset, we dive into the importance of having a positive and proactive mindset regarding sales.

I share with you why I created this book and emphasise how crucial it is to have the right mindset for success. We'll discuss various tools and techniques for developing a positive mindset, such as manifestation, visualisation, goal setting, and gratitude. We'll tackle topics like empathy, overcoming failure, and managing imposter syndrome.

The second pillar, 'Well-being,' is all about taking care of yourself physically, mentally, and emotionally to achieve sustainable success. I'll cover topics like mindfulness, body, confidence, nutrition, therapy, and spiritual well-being. We'll also discuss the importance of having a support system and building a well-being team to help maintain your well-being.

The third and final Pillar, 'Performance,' provides practical advice and techniques for excelling in sales. We'll cover everything from personal branding to the sales process, cold calling, prospecting, and elite salespeople. I'll also provide tips on how to write an effective CV, perform well in an interview, and create a winning 30, 60, and 90-day plan. We'll touch on topics like selling over Zoom, building a board of advisors, and understanding the new buyer.

Overall, my goal with this book is to help you develop a strong sense of confidence and well-being in the sales industry. Whether you need to work through each chapter individually or as a whole, I'm here to guide you every step of the way. By providing practical advice, focusing on building a positive mindset, and taking care of yourself, 'How to Build Sales Confidence' is the ultimate resource for anyone looking to excel in the sales industry. Shall we get started?

Introduction

There are certain secrets and keys to success, and here's the good news—the door *isn't* locked. The only difference is that *only some* are seeking the key. If you're reading this book, however, I'm guessing you possess a growth mindset, and for people like you, I have all the keys here jingling, ready to be taught and implemented. Within these pages are the tools to get you well on your way to becoming successful future sales and business leaders.

Most people will tell you that they 'fell into sales'. For me, it wasn't the case at all. I ran into sales! In my early teens, I discovered books on self-development, business, and autobiographies of successful business people, all of which inspired me to pursue business in my lifetime. When reading these business books, the successful authors often talked about the advantages of learning the sales profession and how it would teach you the power of communication, persuasion, and influencing people. So, I sought out opportunities to develop a skill set in sales while I was at university, preparing me for a career post-university. I found a door-to-door sales job persuading people to get their milk delivered, which was a commission-only role. I would spend about six hours a day invading people's space by knocking on doors on the outskirts of London. Nothing is more personal than knocking on someone's door while they are at home, minding their own business and then trying to sell them milk! That quickly gave me a lesson in *rejection,* which is a fundamental skill in sales. You learn the hard way very quickly when knocking on doors, and most people are telling you to "get lost!"

However, I had a great mentor in the door-to-door milk sales, who taught us to mark a cross for every door we knocked on that told us "no" and to mark a tick when we had a successful outcome. That simple process taught me the power of activity. This great mentor was a fantastic guy called Greg, and his milk business was everything to him, despite milk delivery services being a dying industry. This guy had been ploughing his trade for years to create a lifestyle for himself and his family by recruiting young students like myself to knock on doors in London and convince them to get their milk delivered. He taught me early on to embrace and enjoy the 'no'. The word 'no' is your best friend because the more 'nos' you get, the closer you get to that 'yes'. If you only focus on getting the yes, you will often be disappointed, so you've got to love and enjoy hearing the golden word – 'no!'.

It was a powerful lesson early; most of the time in sales, you hear "no, thank you. No, go away. No, not now. No, it was too expensive. No, I'm not interested". A 'no' can hugely knock your confidence, but if you get a kick out of hearing the word, then it can become an enjoyable experience.

"How do you train yourself to get a kick outta hearing no then?" I asked him.

"It's all about mindset. You must remember that a 'no' is not personal; it's not because someone doesn't like you; it's simply a human reaction to initially being sold to". Said Greg

And it's true; it could be on the door, in a retail store, on the phone, over email, over Zoom, or in person at a trade show—it's an innate human response to respond with a 'no'.

So, in this door-to-door milk sales role, I was excited to practise my craft and learn to demonstrate charisma, confidence, and positive energy the moment someone opened the door (and bear in mind we were trying to convince people to get their milk delivered when 99% of the population picks theirs up at the local supermarket!). We had to develop a sales pattern that persuaded them that it was in their best interests to support their local farmer and dairy and have it delivered, just like in the old days. Greg taught me to walk away only once I had heard 'no' at least three times. It's controversial because, in theory, we are taught from a young age that "no means no", and of course, there are situations where "no" absolutely does mean "no"! But in those sales situations, it takes skill and gall to turn around and say, "well, while I've got you, can I just take a few minutes to explain why I've decided to knock on your door today?"

"No, really, it's not a good time".

"I appreciate what you're saying, but we've got something exciting that will make a difference in how you live your life and support the local community".

"Oh, okay, go on, you seem friendly enough!"

Bingo!

Greg taught me key skills for breaking down sales barriers, building trust, and putting people at ease. He also taught me the art of smiling, and if you ever meet me in person, you'll know I've kept that one up my entire career! Even on the phone, smile because you can hear a smile.

At the same time as the milk sales job, I organised and threw parties at the university and sold tickets to persuade people to come to a nightclub with which I was affiliated. I was a student entrepreneur, all in preparation for a sales and business career. But one night, while I was selling tickets, everything stopped abruptly. I was taken to a mental health hospital and diagnosed with bipolar disorder.

It was humbling and grounding when I realised I had no choice but to accept I was unwell. *This* is where my true journey with confidence began. My illness has led to many highs and lows and multiple hospital admissions. I've continually and consistently had to pick myself up from the bottom, resulting in me losing my confidence and having to rediscover it repeatedly. As a result, I'm well versed in confidence, both in its abundance and absence.

While I hope, dear reader, that you haven't experienced the extreme challenges I've had in my life and career as a result of mental illness, my feeling is that if you have ever lacked confidence or self-belief or are looking to improve your success in sales, this book will hugely benefit you.

Speaking of books, let me explain further how my obsession with sales and business began. I was about

12 years old, and we were on a family holiday to Cyprus with about 20 other families from Windsor; we were such a large clan of Brits that we had taken over an apartment block! One of the other kid's dads was reading books on his sun lounger, and upon further investigation, I saw he was reading a bunch of get-rich-quick books. The guy was a business owner who ran a double-glazing business, and I really admired him. So I asked if I could borrow 'Rich Dad, Poor Dad' from him, and he obliged. The book discusses how important sales is as a fundamental skill, and I was fascinated by the 'secrets' inside. That book sparked my interest in business books, whether sales books or books written by successful people, business owners, and professionals. I became obsessed with the whole literary business world.

Unlike me, most people at school weren't talking about what they wanted to do in the future and had no idea what they would do when they grew up. They were studying, having a good time and doing sport, which I was too, but I was reading books and eating up as much business information as possible in my spare time.

And so, I've come full circle; at 36 years old, I am now releasing my own book on a subject that has completely changed my life for the better – 'Sales Confidence'.

After my diagnosis, I didn't want to be defined as 'a person with a mental illness'. I didn't want someone else's perception of what was and wasn't possible to stop me from achieving the objectives and ambitions I had set for myself. Even though I have a mental illness diagnosis, I was hesitant to accept that I had limitations. When you're diagnosed with bipolar disorder, you're told you shouldn't do anything particularly stressful. They say if you want to be in business, you shouldn't set overly ambitious goals because that might feed your mania, and you shouldn't push yourself to overachieve because that can create stress. I listened and promptly rejected all of the advice. I became determined that, despite the diagnosis, I would still go on to achieve my big ambitions.

To some people, my attitude against the doctor's advice might sound stubborn, but here is my take on it; not everyone can relate to my diagnosis, but we can all agree that we must carve our own pathways. A pathway you have decided upon, not based on what your parents think you should do, how good your manager says you are, your first employer's feedback, or your current friends, because all of the above will evolve and change. You have to believe in yourself and back yourself if you want to be confident that your goals are possible, and you must create your own pathway. I hope that within these pages, you can gain something from my difficult experiences and learn to use confidence to achieve your goals.

Of course, it is not just mental health that can create tangible and invisible barriers to achieving your goals. For example, I learned I would be a first-time father while working my second job after graduation—I was 23 years old. At first, I was scared, and I wondered if it would hurt my chances of success or hinder my ambitions. Instead, I'm glad it made me work even harder to support my new family. It gave me more motivation to be successful

Obstacles don't have to be destructive; we can use them to our advantage. We are much more resilient than we believe ourselves to be.

Why It's Crucial to Master Sales Confidence

A mentee recently asked me, "what does sales confidence look and feel like?" I thought about it for a while, and a strong visual came to mind; I realised that Sales confidence evokes feelings of solidity and strength. It's being able to stand tall and feel so empowered that you know the next thing to come out of your mouth are the right words at the right time that will have the maximum impact. You begin to win when you attain a particular degree of expertise in any endeavour and exhibit confidence in that area. Confidence is a state, and sales confidence is a flow state.

Sales confidence looks solid, powerful, inspiring, engaging, and enthusiastic. When someone is confident, they clearly communicate what, why, and how they wish to convey a message. As a result, if you are the subject of an interaction with that person, you will probably believe what they are telling you. You look and feel sales confidence when you show your expertise and credibility in a clear, articulate, and confident way. Some people might think a confident person is arrogant, but it's not the case. Feeling comfortable and whole makes you more relaxed and naturally more attractive to others. Those around you can sense this level of comfort and solidity, and when someone makes direct eye contact with you, nods along, acknowledges what you're saying, and relates it to you, it makes you feel listened to and trusted. It's important to embrace yourself and present your best self, even if it means not adhering to traditional professional dress codes. I haven't worn a shirt or suit trousers in a professional context in over ten years, yet I still look sharp and put together. Of course, there are appropriate levels of dress for specific contexts, and it's essential to present your best self in a sales context, but ultimately, what you say matters more than what you wear. Confidence is not about arrogance; it's about feeling good in your own skin and presenting your best self to the world.

That's how sales confidence feels to me; what about you?

How does it feel to lack confidence?

Confidence is an inner feeling that you show to others. If you don't feel confident, your body language will show it: your breathing will become shallow, and you might subtly hunch your shoulders, which will squeeze your diaphragm. You might feel smaller, those around you will therefore feel bigger, it will be challenging to get a handle on your words, you might hesitate before you speak, and you will be slower to react to questions. In other words, it's easy for others to notice when we lack confidence!

Lacking confidence is an uncomfortable state that can limit how you approach your interactions with others. Although the signs are subtle, collectively, they mean you are less persuasive, less influential, less powerful, and less impactful. These factors will affect your ability to make progress with someone, especially in the sales cycle or when you're trying to lead a team.

Of course, feeling insecure when you're in a new environment, performing a new task, or learning a new skill is natural, but we can try to break the cycle. As you learn more, you become more skilled, which is a big step toward feeling more confident. Therefore, don't let a lack of confidence intimidate you; it's just a sign that you must work harder to improve yourself and develop your skills.

Working on your confidence is one of the kindest gifts to yourself.

PILLAR ONE

MINDSET

CHAPTER ONE

WHY I CREATED SALES CONFIDENCE

SALES CONFIDENCE is *everything* to me.

I created Sales Confidence because I lacked confidence.

I knew I wasn't the only salesperson who sometimes needed more confidence, so I decided to make a safe place for salespeople to talk about their mental wellbeing and help them flourish. I wanted to create a community of people willing and able to share their authentic selves.

I also launched Sales Confidence as I didn't want myself or others to be judged for mental health reasons; I wanted to be accepted and revered for being a competent and honest salesperson instead. Therefore, I looked for an audience—a tribe, if you will—that would take me for exactly who I am. I'd been to many mental health meetups but didn't click with many people because they didn't share my interests, which are primarily business and motivation. I don't last long in environments without an opportunity to discuss ambition.

So, to counter that, I created an environment where like-minded, motivated business and salespeople could spend time together, share their stories, and express themselves. **That environment is Sales Confidence.** There is now a safe space for people to talk about their challenges, mental health, and how they feel about themselves without judgement, and it's a massive win for the industry.

Sales Confidence has become the go-to resource for people who want to gain confidence in their sales careers. It's the trusted starting point to guide individuals to any help they may need. While there are many sales gurus out there who assert their personalities and claim to 'know it all', I recognise that I may have some, but not all, of the answers. However, I have a wealth of experience and stories that can guide aspiring entrepreneurs. I sell every day, but I don't oversee complex sales processes or manage massive sales teams like many who attend my events do. Instead, my role in this industry is in service to my peers.

I have built a solid personal brand and have a lot of connections to influential sales leaders in the sales community. I aim to identify talented sales leaders and tell their stories through Sales Confidence, and act as their megaphone to boost their brands. Sales Confidence is a destination for people to learn about sales and sales leaders from other people; it is the place where individuals can find all the resources they need to succeed in their sales careers and the gateway to everything else, providing individuals with videos, events, memberships, and information about influential people in the sales community. Predominantly, however, Sales Confidence is a safe space to be open about your vulnerabilities.

Despite my diagnosis, I don't want to be considered unwell—I don't want to live like that. **So, each day, I think of myself as progressive, disciplined, positive, and focused on the opportunities ahead, so I can continue to be happy and successful.** *That* is how I want to be perceived. So, I made Sales Confidence so that other people and I could talk about our problems without being made to feel like we were inadequate. Instead, we can inspire others and give back because Sales Confidence is an environment that allows people to express their authentic selves.

Sales Confidence is about much more than being the best salesperson.

While I was motivated to set up my own business, it was challenging to brand it correctly at first, and I had many different variations of the name going around my mind and notepad: 'Elite Sales,' 'Sales Dictators,' 'Sales Superstars,' and 'This Sale and That Sale.'

I wanted a word that summed up mental health; the word 'confidence' really spoke to me. 'Confidence' changes depending on how you perceive your life and can thus have positive and negative connotations. I've gone from lacking confidence to being overly confident, which sounds great but can be detrimental if it goes too far. It can be a delicate balance.

Once I cemented the 'Sales Confidence' brand, hearing other people's definitions of sales confidence over the years has been insightful. For example, one person might say that a confident salesperson is loyal, dependable, and does what they say. Another is that someone with sales confidence has a can-do attitude and gets on with things. Others say that those who have sales confidence have an appetite for winning. Sales confidence, among many other things, sees humility as an advantage and tries to help others.

Sales confidence means admitting your weaknesses and strengths and still feeling good about yourself.

CHAPTER TWO

MANIFESTATION, VISUALISATION, AND GOAL SETTING

I'M A BIG BELIEVER in manifestation. I have seen it work in my own life, and it has dramatically impacted how confident I feel about new projects and goals. This chapter is here to empower you with a transformative tool for boosting your confidence and achieving your goals. I firmly believe in its impact. Manifestation has elevated my confidence and aided me in embarking on new projects, chasing my dreams, and has significantly boosted my confidence by reshaping my self-perception and approach to goals.

Visualisation also plays a vital role, encouraging you to picture your desired outcomes and success. This mental imagery motivates and deepens your belief in your ability to achieve your dreams by replacing limiting beliefs with empowering thoughts and affirmations. This mental rewiring promotes self-belief and is a stronghold in confidence building.

Staying committed and focused on your goals is another manifestation principle. Dedication cultivates discipline, which is closely tied to confidence. Achieving your manifested goals creates a positive feedback loop, solidifying self-assurance.

Manifestation also helps counteract the negativity bias by replacing negative thoughts with positive ones. Your self-talk transforms, leading to a more positive and confident internal dialogue.

So, how?

You, too, can manifest your desired life by visualising your goals, successes, and achievements. Before you think I've lost the plot and am about to impart a bunch of new-age nonsense' (not my belief), please bear with me. In society, the concept of 'manifestation' is dressed in various guises; some say it's the universe working in your favour, some say it is the fabric of creation, and some say it's simply a matter of biology. I agree with the latter. Manifestation is teaching your subconscious mind to change its beliefs and limits. This significantly affects how you live your life and whether you will succeed. By rewiring your brain, you can make your thoughts come true by teaching your subconscious brain to follow the breadcrumbs your conscious brain has been leaving. It's all about focus; the more you focus on something, the more your subconscious will start working towards it. Be careful, however, as this works for negatively focused thoughts too! There is a notion called 'the negativity bias', meaning the brain will more readily latch on to negative ideas and musings. The negativity bias comes from when we were a younger species, and the world was much more dangerous for us. Thus, we are more likely to see a negative situation than a positive one because it used to be a matter of life and death. Arguably, the world is much safer, but we are still hardwired to see the negative in most situations.

Positive thoughts and actions, on the other hand, can overcome the negativity bias, though it may take some getting used to. An excellent way to begin the process is to make sure your focus is always on the positive outcome. If you find yourself musing and fearing a lousy outcome about a situation, recognise that you are doing it and switch the thought into a positive one.

The Manifestation Method—Visualisation.

Let's conduct a rudimentary thought experiment. Your brain is a passenger waiting for a train, and the train is your mindset. The manifestation method trains (pardon the pun!) your brain to get on the correct train with the right people, with the right motives, at the right time. The manifestation method can get you to any desired outcome, goal, or destination, but first, you must learn to **visualise**. Visualisation is easier for some than others, but like anything, you can learn to become good at it. Visualisation works by creating an image or a movie in the mind of your desired outcome. Let's try a visualisation right now. Try to picture the following scene in your head.

You're waiting for a train on an outdoor platform in London. It's 8 am, you've had a great sleep, and it's a beautiful sunny spring morning. There is a young man in a suit, and he nervously asks you, "Excuse me, is the next train the correct one to Brighton? I've never caught this train before".

"Yes, it is! It will take you straight there, and the journey is around one hour and five minutes". You reply.

Next, the train pulls up, and you find a cosy window seat, the young man finds his seat three aisles down, and in one hour and five minutes, you pull into Brighton station. The young man looks over at you, smiles, and mouths, "thanks", and you walk out of the station into a perfect spring day.

Was the warm sunlight coming through the train window palpable? Could you imagine how the young man who asked about the train looked? When he inquired whether the train was the right one, did you feel confident in your response? If the answer is no, reread it, and imagine yourself in the scene.

A big part of manifestation is visualising an experience as if it has already happened; after all, how can you get somewhere if you can't imagine where you're going? In addition, practising visualisation can build muscle memory and help your subconscious map out a route.

I constantly visualise in colour and am very accurate when imagining all the specifics and emotions related to that goal. For example, if the goal is to improve my body's shape and overall physical health, I visualise myself looking in the mirror and being extremely happy with what I see. If I can clearly visualise that version of myself, whether it's a slimmer, stronger, or more fit version, my subconscious will focus on that when I work out. I keep that concrete image of what I want to accomplish and move toward in my head while I'm working out, and I strongly visualise the scene, so I can bring it into reality and inspire myself to workout harder. If you prefer to physically see your ideal outcome, you can post an image to your phone or tape it on your bathroom mirror.

But, as we are not here to talk about my physique all day, let's discuss visualisation from a business, sales and confidence perspective. As you may be aware, in sales, we have 'sales kickoff', 'annual kickoff', and 'quarterly reviews'. So, let's try a different experiment utilising the same visualisation strategies discussed above. First, play it out as if your quarterly review is tomorrow. Are you the subject of favourable remarks? Are you getting a happy response from people? Are those around you expressing their gratitude to you? Are your team members smiling and shaking your hand? If the answer to these questions is 'no', 'maybe', or 'I don't know', you might want to try the above manifestation technique.

Sit down and create an image or a movie of how you would like the quarterly review to play out. Do you want to win salesperson of the quarter? Would you like to achieve a record-breaking quarter? Would you like to experience championing from your colleagues? Whatever your ideal scenario is, imagine yourself walking into the review with your desired outcome playing out in front of you. *How do you feel?* Imagine yourself smiling; Imagine the thrill you would feel. Think about the confidence you'll experience once you achieve your desired goals. While visualising, you can imagine a whole world and walk around in this new, ever more confident identity you're creating. Consider adding colour to make it seem more realistic, and pay close attention to how you are feeling. How does it make you feel when people admire your achievements? How does it feel to be on stage accepting an award for the top salesperson? How does it make you feel to overachieve your target at the end of the year? For the best results in a visualisation, examine all of your senses. Watch the crowd as you accept the award, feel the big, fat cheque within your fingertips, and listen to your cheering peers. Visualisation, like any technique, can be improved and honed with practice, so make time for daily visualisation. You can use visualisation in any area of your life; the most crucial element is doing it regularly. My motto is 'if you can visualise it, it will hugely improve your chances of getting there.' It is an easy practice that will stimulate a hugely positive outcome.

I also practise mindfulness daily, as it helps calm my inner self, builds confidence, and lets me take stock of my feelings. For example, when I'm done working out, I often take five to ten minutes to calm down by taking deep breaths. If you're new to mindfulness, "box breathing" is a simple technique.

Box Breathing

Inhale for a count of 6, hold your breath for a count of 6, exhale for a count of 6, and hold for a count of 6. Repeat until you feel more relaxed. Breathing this way is a form of meditation, but I don't always think of it that way; for me, it's a moment to slow down my mind and release any tension I may be holding onto. This is also an excellent time to work on your visualisation. Once you have meditated, released any tension, and taken stock of how you feel, you can take a few minutes visualising how you wish your following meeting, day, month, or year to be. Think big about what you truly want, and imagine yourself in the scene. This will increase your confidence by making you feel like you have already arrived at your desired place. If you're sceptical of visualisation, why not try it for a week? It only takes 30 seconds, and who knows—it could completely change your life.

Affirmations

Affirmations can help us learn how to quieten negativity and start living more positively. Negativity is a part of life; although we can't eliminate it, we can alter our reactions.

Affirmations and positive self-talk are potent tools for overcoming negativity. We need to repeat positive statements silently or out loud to begin changing our thoughts. **Well-word affirmations can significantly impact a person's sense of self, sense of agency, and view of the world.**

You have the power to create the life you want, and by affirming this to yourself every day, you will start to live that truth. You will accomplish more and have less difficulty getting where you want to go if you have a positive and joyful attitude. You will pursue your goals, triumph over adversity, and look forward to the future. A happy life depends on having a positive outlook, which is why positive affirmations work so well. So if you want a good life, repeat these optimistic statements, and of course, feel free to write your own! You may use them when your mood is dipping, especially on the worst days.

1. **I will nourish my mind and body healthily.**
   Making time for self-care is an investment in your happiness. You should fuel your body with healthy foods and engage in frequent physical

activity. You'll feel happier in your everyday life if you spend some time each day working on yourself, physically and mentally.

2. **I improve myself every day.**
   You may fill your cup with positivity by reminding yourself how you grow and improve daily.

3. **I'm confident in my right to success.**
   Believing in yourself and your worth opens you up to receiving extraordinary opportunities. You're now ready to quit settling and start saying "yes" solely to the genuinely beneficial opportunities.

4. **I refuse to give any credence to the criticisms against me.**
   It would be best to only care about what you think of yourself. All that counts is whether or not *you* like yourself.

5. **I'll *practise* tranquillity and tolerance.**
   Happiness comes from inner calm and acceptance of what you can't alter.

6. **I believe in my abilities and am dedicated to realising my potential.**
   If you put your mind to it, you can do anything

7. **I am in charge of my pleasure. Therefore, I will make the decisions that bring me joy.**
   You are the only one who can make you happy mentally and emotionally.

8. **It's in my power to have success and fulfilment.**
   If you feel like you're losing steam, repeat this affirmation to yourself, and it'll give you the boost you need to keep going.

9. **I choose to associate with upbeat and optimistic people.**
   You tend to pick up the attitudes of people closest to you, whether favourable or harmful. So get rid of the toxic individuals in your life with this encouraging affirmation.

10. **With each challenge I overcome, I emerge more powerful than before.**
    Keep in mind that overcoming adversity builds character.

11. **There's time for me to finish it.**
    Anxiety might set in when one feels pressed for time. If you worry excessively about this, try saying this affirmation to yourself.

12. **I patiently await my hopes and desires to be realised.**
    It will take time for the things you want to happen, so convince yourself that you are patient and can enjoy working toward your goals.

13. **I don't take any of my accomplishments for granted.**
    When you value yourself, you can't help but feel good.
    Try these affirmations daily and see how you feel after a week.

Pick Your People

Being around happy, positive people will make you feel better and give you more energy, boosting your confidence. Conversely, negative individuals drain your strength and happiness and are likely to give your confidence a huge hit. Whether they are relatives, coworkers, or acquaintances, you can protect yourself from their negative energy for a happier life. How would you rate your current level of energy? Do you make the most of each day or just get by? Being around a lot of pessimists might have a depressing effect.

Try these strategies if you want to stop feeling drained by negative individuals.

- **Don't try to change people.**
  Many pessimists have been thinking about their problems for so long that it has become a comforting routine. They will only improve their outlook and circumstances once they are ready and have the desire to do so. Trying to alter other people is a pointless use of your limited resources.

- **Recognise your strengths and shortcomings.**
  Those who maintain an optimistic view are the ones who can give themselves a fair assessment. Humans all have flaws, so it's good to be aware of them and work to fix them.

- **Shift your attention back to the task at hand.**
  How can you stay sane amid a tornado of cynics? You might be unable to alter the circumstances,

but you have control over your outlook. Try to have a more optimistic view of things rather than giving in to pessimism.

- **Define limits.**
  Setting limits may make you happier and more energetic, no matter what kind of person influences your life. Unfortunately, we will always encounter negative individuals, but they can only push us as far as we let them.

  Boundaries in a relationship, whether personal or professional, are your right. Gain confidence in your ability to say no and observe its impact. You don't have to take people's negativity on yourself or act as a doormat. Even though you may want to help others, you cannot resolve all of their problems. Instead of worrying about what others want, put your needs first for a change. You are not selfish just because you care about yourself and put your wants first.

- **Spend time with upbeat individuals.**
  Isn't it amazing how much light a candle can cast in a dark room? Likewise, positivity drives away pessimism. The key to a happy life is surrounding oneself with upbeat, optimistic individuals. A positive environment will swiftly shut down a negative individual.

- **Let go.**
  When you're feeling down and stressed out, your mind may wander to the effects of bad things that have happened in the past. You give your

negative ideas power over your life when you give them your undivided attention. Although it may seem impossible, you have total control over your mind and life.

CHAPTER THREE
BELIEF SYSTEMS AND VALUES

BELIEF SYSTEMS and values profoundly impact confidence by shaping your self-perception and guiding your actions. When you hold beliefs that align with self-worth and capability, you naturally feel more confident in your abilities. Similarly, when your values align with your goals and aspirations, your actions become more purpose-driven, reinforcing self-belief. These belief systems and values provide a strong foundation for decision-making and goal pursuit, resulting in inner strength.

Your beliefs and values are the bedrock of your motivation and drive, positively and directly affecting your confidence. As a result, your most firmly held beliefs and values will guide your daily actions and routines at work; this is who you are. Therefore, gaining a deeper understanding of your core values and belief system can help you improve or change your daily life.

At the beginning of your career, you might put a lot of weight on how much money you make from a sales job. Therefore, "are you money motivated?" is the number one interview question. Employers are curious about this, as your response indicates your level of ambition and appetite to put in additional effort. If you are paid based on your performance, your pay will be related to your actions.

So, how much of an emphasis do finances have in your life? Are finances a significant motivating factor? Of course, as you get better at your job, your earnings will become more stable, and you'll reach a point where you're happy and comfortable with your finances. But this then begs the question, "How much do you value assisting others and advancing their careers?"

It's essential to give back to the industry that has helped me so much, and that's a major motivating factor for me. I am willing to assist others because of this fundamental principle. Of course, it helps to have the correct values, procedures, and frameworks to become a great seller, but let's look at how one's philosophy influences one's professional methods.

Thought Experiment

Ask yourself, what negative beliefs do you believe about yourself? They might look like this:

"I'm not good enough."

"I won't hit my target."

Whatever negative beliefs you might have, you can turn a negative into a positive by using the affirmations and visualisations we discussed in the previous chapter.

In its "Statement of Values", a company writes down the core beliefs that drive it and serve as a guide for how it deals with customers, workers, suppliers, investors, and the general public. Still, it's up to the company's owners to determine what matters most to their enterprise. For example, one of their core principles might be that they think all of their clients should be treated fairly. Also included is their opinion on the need for a healthy work-life balance for all employees.

But what has this got to do with me?

As solopreneurs, individuals, and salespeople, we can think about our own "statement of values" and begin to think deeply about our principles. It's essential to know our boundaries and understand our own compass.

In times of adversity, a person's core values and beliefs come into play. For example, if a company's gym product caused injury and the associated value was "The wellbeing of our customers is the most important thing", the company would immediately recall all affected products, stop production, find out what went wrong, and set up a customer plan. In contrast, the same business would conduct itself less responsibly if "customer wellbeing" wasn't one of its stated values.

Beliefs alter the way we lead our lives.

If you think you're not talented, you will start to believe it, making it difficult to take advantage of opportunities, improve situations, and strengthen relationships. Business practices are driven by people, and the constraints and obstacles are also enacted there. Therefore this list might be rather long, depending on the specific environment. For example, if a person believes they don't have enough time, it becomes the guiding principle by which they live their life. We must implement change if our beliefs need to be revised for growth.

When it comes to making business decisions, how do values factor in?

Many people make empty claims about their fundamental values, only reflecting the image they wish to present to the public rather than the values by which they do business. While these statements may have some validity, many companies today engage in situational ethics, making lofty claims while doing nothing to put them into effect. For example, simply declaring support for charity is meaningless. While it's admirable to do so when flush with cash, many people struggle to make ends meet and aren't able to give a significant percentage to charity, even if they want to. While their intentions are good, they must live up to their own standards.

The finest businesses extensively study their founding principles before making public statements. They observe unfavourable tendencies and make personnel adjustments to get it back where they believe it should be before publicly announcing their core beliefs. As individual salespeople, we should do the same.

Beliefs should be expressed through actions rather than words. Unfortunately, this is the typical blunder business owners make—they often issue positive sound bites, but their actions have never matched their words. For example, one of the biggest tricks a corporation can use to make you believe it stands for something it doesn't is to use a slogan like "we stand for..". when in reality, the firm doesn't stand for anything. It is essential as solo entities; we don't follow suit; once trust is lost, so is business.

I am sceptical of people who make bold claims about who they are. On the other hand, people who do the right thing quietly, without announcing it, have my full attention. Again I want to emphasise the importance of reading about others and listening to podcasts or interviews of people you admire. This can give you inspiration for your belief systems. We should be reviewing our beliefs monthly, quarterly and yearly. There's so much going on in your mind impacting your output that it's imperative to reflect on self-talk and your beliefs. You're just drifting through your career if you don't do this.

It's the same as knowing that exercising and eating healthily will improve your life—the facts are obvious, and there are millions of different variations on the same concept. Essentially, if you burn more than you eat, you lose weight; those are the fundamental facts. So, in the same way, despite knowing that goal setting will significantly improve your success, 80% of people still won't bother. But why? I have some theories on this. If you're trying to get somewhere in your car, you set the destination in GPS, and you get there, but with career goals, I think many people run on blind faith.

Most people must realise how powerful and intentional they can be to change their lives. People reach a certain level of earnings, which is more than they ever expected, yet don't know they reached it and thus can't think beyond that. Some people are surprised that they've reached a point in their life and career and believe there is nothing more to achieve.

Question: Why do we ignore fundamental truths and stop trying to achieve more? There are truths, such as the fact that if you read the right books and surround yourself with the right people, you will begin to think like the words you read and the people you speak to, that you attract the things you think about and the actions you take, and that you will attract like-minded people. Finding these truths only takes a little digging, but so many people fail to use them. I don't want to take any political stances on society, but obviously, we're part of a machine. If most people are happy with £35,000 per year, we'll stop striving, shut up, and consume what is being fed to us.

As I've pursued wealth creation, riches, and success, I began to think, "why doesn't everyone want to do the same?" But, I concluded that society wouldn't function if everybody wanted to be the top dog. If you think of society as a beehive, some of us make honey, some protect the queen, yet very few are *the* queen! Regardless of our upbringing, some people simply aren't strivers. However, if you are a striver and have a growth mindset (and if you're reading this book, you are!), you can quickly learn the fundamental codes that will drive you to success. If you invest enough time to learn the secrets to success (and implement them), it's almost impossible to fail.

CHAPTER FOUR

GRATITUDE AND BUILDING CONFIDENCE WITH OTHERS

SALES CONFIDENCE IS GRATITUDE IN ACTION

Gratitude

IN SALES, gratitude is essential—it will boost confidence and improve performance overall. When you have gratitude, you focus on what you have instead of what you lack. This can help you develop a more positive outlook and increase your overall satisfaction with your job.

Also, you need to believe in yourself and your product or service to convince others to buy from you successfully, and when you are grateful, you can focus on the positive aspects of your job and product or service. This can help you develop a sense of pride in what you're selling, which can, in turn, boost your confidence.

Furthermore, expressing gratitude can help you build stronger relationships with your customers. When you take the time to thank your customers for their business, they feel appreciated and valued. This can increase their loyalty to you and your company, leading to more sales in the long run.

All that being said, practising gratitude does not come easily to many people, especially when you're starting to feel the weight of hearing 'no' all the time. Do you find it challenging to find the silver lining in any given situation, or do you feel there's nothing to be thankful for? What if I were to tell you *that this is why* you have such a hard time with everything? Knowing gratitude's power and how to use it to reach your goals is beneficial. I'm 36 now and appreciate practising gratitude, but I didn't think about any of this in my teens or twenties, and wow, I wish I had!

Gratitude Exercise:

Stop for a moment, pause, and take 20 seconds to reflect on everything you are grateful for. That might be your career, family, pets, car, health, etc. Appreciate where you are in life. What does it feel like? If you find yourself thinking about what you are lacking, ignore those feelings right now and instead focus on what you ***do*** *have. That could be the air you breathe or your good health. Reflect in the present on everything in your life that you are grateful for; family, friendships, your current career status, whatever it is in that moment. Appreciate where you are right now in your life and embrace what it feels like. Again, if you feel like you lack some things in life, put those aside for a moment and focus on what you have and are grateful for.*

Stopping and pausing to practise gratitude will increase your energy levels and motivate you. Whatever challenge or obstacle you face, there is almost always a way to overcome it, especially if you are a high-performance-minded individual seeking to do more.

It's essential to be grateful for who you are today, to recognise that you are valuable, and to be thankful for your experiences. Research shows that if you perceive your life with gratitude, you will begin to see more positivity in your life. Again, this comes back to the law of attraction—what you think, you attract. Gratitude attracts good things into our lives, which is why we should express gratitude and show appreciation when people inspire or help us. The more we express gratitude and appreciation for ourselves, others, and what we have today, the more we'll be able to appreciate what we get next. It would be unfortunate if we reached our goal without mindfully appreciating what we had accomplished while working towards it. If we lived like that, we might constantly move on to future goals and never experience our achievements. We should relish in our accomplishments, as they will help us think positively and attract more success into our lives.

In the past, I would frequently fail to express how grateful I was for a favourable situation, allowing it to go under my emotional radar and deprive me of the satisfaction of accomplishment. I've subsequently learnt to be more mindful of these things, and I'm happier and more productive as a result. If you are enjoying the results of your labour, you are more inclined to work harder the following day, week, month, or year.

Here are some methods to practise gratitude:

- Keep a gratitude journal (write a list of 5-10 things you are grateful for every morning).
- Saying affirmations in your head (I am grateful for my health, I am grateful for the roof over my head, I am grateful for my partner/friends/family, I am grateful for that sale, etc.).
- Get used to saying "thank you" to others more often. The more you are mindful of what you are grateful for, the more you will feel motivated to push further and succeed.

Anyone can benefit from cultivating a more grateful attitude. Once you learn to appreciate what you already have, you'll be astounded at how quickly your life can change for the better. For starters, being a happier and more giving person makes you more attractive to success and prosperity. Being thankful regularly has been shown to increase happiness, and happy people are more likely to accomplish their daily goals as they are more motivated, creative, and **confident.**

Gratitude improves your state of mind, heart, soul, and body.

Our physical, mental, emotional, and spiritual wellness must be balanced. When you're feeling down, it's probably because your vibrational frequency is at an all-time low, and your negativity levels are through the roof. Spending a little time every day looking for things to be thankful for can make a big difference in all parts of your life. Consider people constantly exuding confidence and positive emotions; they are less likely to become ill, have a bad day, or fail (not that failure is always bad, but more later). When you have a good mindset and believe you can do anything, you attract good things into your life.

People often assume that money, cars, clothes, and houses, define their level of success, but that's not the case. In fact, excess money can lead to more problems if you do not manage it properly, as greed and selfishness can be destructive. Learn to appreciate what you have now to be more prepared to take care of and maintain what you receive in the future. Your mind will thank you for it, and it will be easier to keep up your confidence. In the same way, your body and mind will be grateful, and it will be easier to keep your confidence.

Gratitude Will Help You Focus on Your Manifestation

One way gratitude improves your life is by shifting your focus from one area of your life to another. When you think about it, our life is what we choose to concentrate on. It is natural to allow all of the negative things that happen in your life to receive your undivided attention, but we should try and negate this. Have faith in your efforts, and be thankful for the opportunity to learn from your mistakes. Even if an outcome is less than ideal, you can still be grateful for the experience, and when you approach the most challenging problems with a positive perspective, it will be much easier to handle them. Of course, this won't happen overnight, and it might take time to rewire your mind to think differently. Still, taking even small steps and trying to see things from a different point of view can lead to big changes.

I cannot overstate how important your mindset is in determining your outcomes.

Reduces your fixation on your deepest fears

Being grateful alters your mental state by presenting you with a new mindset. Nothing terrible lasts forever, and when you learn to recognise the things in life for which you are grateful, things like failures, disappointments, and those crippling anxieties that keep you awake at night lose their influence over your mind. Fears usually centre on the possibility of losing something or not being good enough. It could be love, money, security, or anything else you've conjured up in your subconscious mind. With gratitude, you produce abundance when you appreciate what you have.

Encourages you to achieve your goals and objectives

Most successful people say that goal setting is essential. This is because plans provide your thoughts with purpose and a clear path. Your subconscious mind will only recognise your aspirations if you have a concrete goal. Gratitude is essential for goal setting and achievement because they complement each other perfectly. To make something happen, whether in a week, a month, or a year, you must devise a strategy for putting it into action and making it a reality. When you incorporate thankfulness into your goal-setting process, you can stay focused on what you want to happen and avoid procrastination.

People constantly striving to advance, such as salespeople like you, have attitudes focused on growth and development, and they recognise the need to give appreciation at each milestone. The goal of gratitude is to identify things in your life and endeavours for which you are grateful and build on them to improve your circumstances. Try to avoid remaining stagnant and not striving for growth – there is nothing worse than a person who is unwilling to grow. The universe only has two modes: "grow and "decay", so you'll either be expanding or rotting, metaphorically speaking.

Start a daily ritual, beginning in the morning, of listing things for which you are grateful to advance your goals and achieve your desired level. Even if it's just a few details or something as simple as existing, begin doing this every day before you leave for work or start your daily effort toward achieving sales success.

Taking even tiny steps and attempting to see things from a fresh perspective will result in fantastic transformations.

I've already talked about how thankfulness may help you improve emotionally, physically, spiritually, and psychologically. When you successfully shift your attitude to begin thinking more positively, you will experience a stronger sense of clarity and a zen-like peace of mind, regardless of what is happening. We've all been through things that can throw us off track, make us feel uneasy, mess with our minds, and wear us out, but a little gratitude (for the life lessons!) can lighten a heavy heart.

Gratitude can provide a sense of fulfilment that leads to the realisation that you have more than enough, which leaves you less stressed and more confident.

Gratitude provides you with peace of mind and freedom from worry, resulting in greater confidence.

Empathy

People often have the wrong idea that being confident means putting others down to make yourself look better. This is completely incorrect. Instead, in order to truly feel confident, we should try to understand how others feel. We've all encountered people who are less fortunate than us: those who don't have a spare set of clothes, are unemployed, or don't have friends or family to support them. From a human standpoint, even though it is difficult to relate to others, you can cultivate empathy by treating everyone with respect. I'm not showing empathy if I'm wandering around in Hugo Boss clothes avoiding others less fortunate or speaking out of turn, such as boasting about money or whining about my job. Wherever possible, we should strive to get on someone's level and try to grasp what they feel and experience from their perspective and their frame of reference.

This philosophy of empathy is absolutely essential in sales. In sales, you've typically got a product or service that is supposed to solve another person's problem, but, how can you support a customer and meet them on an emotional level when you don't understand what they're going through in their business or how their problems are impacting them? If you can empathise with their situation and understand their problem, you are much more likely to be able to solve it. People want to feel listened to and understood, and you can only do that by actively listening and then reflecting back to them what you've heard. This demonstrates that you're empathising with their situation.

Empathy is a hugely overlooked factor in sales and one that I implore you to practise.

Safe Environment

If you're new to sales, this portion might not immediately benefit you, but as you move up the ladder into leadership positions, knowing about a 'safe environment' will hugely increase confidence within your sales team. **A safe environment is simply a space where you won't be judged for expressing yourself.** The best human-to-human interaction in a secure environment I've experienced has been in therapy, and the great thing about a therapist is there is zero judgement about the words coming out of your mouth.

This 'no judgement space' is also a great solution in a sales environment. Sales can be a stressful career, and it's important that salespeople have an opportunity to air their feelings. A manager must work to create a safe environment that offers the salesperson an opportunity to share all of the challenges they're facing, the scary calls they have scheduled, be open about their fears, and feel able to ask for support. If there isn't a safe environment and the salesperson doesn't feel comfortable expressing themselves, they're less likely to approach somebody and speak up when they need help. A safe environment is a protected place where you can ask for help, share your challenges without judgement, and be supported correctly. If you are a manager, or a salesperson within an organisation, it is worth implementing a safe environment if one doesn't already exist.

A Framework for Creating a Safe Environment:

1. The first to consider is the physical space you will use. It should be an enclosed room with no distractions. It's okay for a room to be windowless, like an interior room, so the person-to-person interaction is entirely focused on the individual. This environment invites individuals to open up and share.

2. Create a safe space psychologically. Tell the person that you won't judge them and that the conversation will be kept private. They must be comforted that anything said in the space is between the two individuals and not to be repeated outside. They must trust the other person will be there and listen, and the focus here is on *active listening*. So again, there is no judgement, just sharing opinions, providing guidance, and helping the individual within the safe space to share the challenges and experiences they might be facing.

3. Informing the individual to keep an open mind and to not be afraid of their own emotions. Assure them that this is a trusted and confidential space.

4. Focus on the emotion. If you're creating the space for another individual, have patience

and be a good listener. That means keeping your lips sealed, letting the other person take their time, being thoughtful and transparent in your questions, and allowing the individual to respond. For example, you might ask, "what do you hope is the best outcome of the challenge? How do you feel about the current experience?" Concentrate on the answers, which will unlock the individual's emotions rather than just the practicalities. You're trying to connect with the person at a deeper level so that you can understand their experience and the scenario impacting their emotion.

5. Reassurance and comfort. Once someone's disclosed or shared something personal, you see underneath and draw back the curtain. That's when you will realise an issue at work might not necessarily be triggered by something in the workplace. It could, instead, be triggered by something going on in somebody's life, and they've now trusted you with that information. You told them earlier that they should have trust in you, and now you must show and demonstrate that trust in how you have taken on that information. Please give them the confidence that the information is safe with you unless there are serious actions to be taken. *However, those actions should only be taken with the permission of the person involved.*

CHAPTER FIVE

DEALING WITH SUCCESS AND FAILURE HEALTHILY

SUCCESS MEANS different things to different people. However, the main thing for everybody is that *success has to be sustainable.* I learned that the hard way and suffered burnout. Let me share a personal experience that taught me a valuable lesson. I used to be entirely consumed by pursuing success in my early career. I thought the only way to get ahead was to work myself to the bone, which seemed to be paying off.

But one day, everything came crashing down. The constant stress and pressure led to burnout, and before I knew it, I was in the hospital for weeks. It was a wake-up call that made me realise that my approach to success was not sustainable and took a serious toll on my mental and physical health.

Taking time out to recover from burnout was a frustrating experience. I felt like I was wasting precious time that could have been spent working towards my goals. But looking back, I now understand that the time spent focusing on my mental and physical health was far from wasted. Instead, it taught me the importance of self-care and balance, a lesson I will carry with me for the rest of my life.

Sustainability means that you can maintain your success rate. Each success should add a feel-good factor to your day, week, month, or year. Break down goals into smaller milestones to keep success positivity and a sense of accomplishment going.

What's the point of being successful?

If you don't feel good about your success, what's the point of being successful? Again, this comes back to goal setting, visualisation, and being mindful of what success means to you.

When you are successful, don't overlook it and miss out on the feeling of that success. Instead, enjoy the experience as you go along.

Burnout

Success must be sustainable. It's not sustainable to overwork to achieve your goals, burn out, and then become ill due to achieving those goals. Sustainable success is when you achieve your goals and feel good mentally and physically as a result. In many cases, the things we consider to be "success" in our lives are actually the things that are making us ill and unsuccessful in other areas of our lives, and this is frequently referred to as material success. If all you focus on is acquiring material possessions, the feel-good factor will last for a much shorter period of time.

Think of the young salespeople working overtime towards their first watch, car, or house. They finally get there, but the joy is short-lived, and then they need more significant material gains, and the cycle never ends. In general, questions about long-term success should include: are you healthy? Are you grateful for what you've got? Do you appreciate what's around you?

Unhealthy Success

When an inflated ego gets involved, particularly in our Western world, we can become attached to material outcomes and believe they will make us feel better about ourselves. But in reality, obsession with material gain can shorten a person's life and make it harder to feel real happiness. Of course, we should shoot for the money, but only if we have a strong foundation of health, and happiness to sustain it.

Overcoming Failure

I've always been overly ambitious and have set what I call 'stretch goals', many of which I have failed to achieve in my lifetime. One of those examples of a stretch goal was in my rowing career, and one of my primary goals was to represent Great Britain. Plenty of my peers were representing Great Britain, so it wasn't a hugely unattainable goal, but it meant a lot to me. Unfortunately, I didn't reach that goal, and it hurt me deeply that I couldn't play my favourite sport for my country. In spite of this, I've always believed that my failure to achieve my rowing goal served as motivation for my success in other areas of my life!

There's a positive aspect about significant failures that can drive you on in future endeavours, not least because you don't want to repeat the experience. I've also had several business failures where I set out to achieve specific goals and failed because I was overly ambitious in those goals. However, my advice is that you must weather the storm and not become too emotionally tied to your goals. Goals change, and you can pivot on your goals, but your health and well-being and your association with those goals are what matter. When I was younger, I used to get depressed if I didn't accomplish the goals I set for myself, but I have since learned that this isn't the way. Instead, you need to pick yourself up, brush yourself down and strive to try and hit the next goal in front of you. You can't change the past, but can change the future.

I think there are two sides to failure, the downside and the upside. If you focus on the upside, failure can inspire you to attain new goals, push yourself in other endeavours, springboard towards the right path and help you pivot in the right direction.

Your Inner Voice

Your inner voice is vital in all aspects of business, especially in sales. At times, my inner voice can be my best friend and others, my worst enemy. I can't speak for others, but I believe many of us have an inner voice and dialogue that we converse with daily. That voice allows us to set a path and get through the tasks we have set out to do each day, and that voice can be very positive, but often it can be damaging and put us down. The voice may nitpick at things it believes you could improve, and if you're not mindful of the voice and how it's impacting you, it can garner too much control, create adverse outcomes, and become very damaging.

It's better to become friends with the voice and be aware of it. Your inner voice is your subconscious mind directing you, but if you don't know how to control it, it might lead you astray and impair your ability to carry out plans. I am pretty introspective regarding my inner voice and spend a lot of time reflecting on what it says. First, I think about whether it's helping me in a good way, and if it isn't, I break bad habits by reminding myself that I am in charge. Remember, when the negative thoughts come, to remind yourself that you are a good person, that you are kind, that other people care about you, that you are unique, and so are others. It's important to remember to treat yourself with kindness and look after yourself—that's a crucial part of understanding your inner voice. We need to learn how to control our inner voices so that they don't negatively affect us when things are stressful or when we are under pressure to perform. Understanding the dialogue in your mind is essential, and you should counter it with positivity when needed. Similarly, don't be discouraged when it's hostile to you; as previously discussed, we can say positive things to ourselves that rewire any negative bias to empower the mind.

I would recommend keeping a diary and writing down your inner voice so that you can get a visual and a handle on the discussion within your mind. It begins to bring the inner world to life, so you can observe and start feeding yourself more positivity. Sometimes, introspective reflection on that voice can be difficult to counter because a stream of consciousness doesn't always make much sense. Keep in mind that voice is there to lead you, defend you, and prepare you for situations you may encounter. Nevertheless, it's not always the best guide, so if you see that stream of consciousness on a page in front of you, you can begin to realise what's being said about you and how you perceive yourself. Then you can think about counter-acting that with positivity and forcing yourself into a brighter outlook. When people say 'fake it until you make it', they are saying that you need to feed yourself with positivity, and thus, you will develop your belief system more positively. It makes a huge difference.

Managing Your Ego

My definition of ego is 'I' and "myself". There are lots of arguments about what it means, but in the general lexicon, it means how you identify with yourself. Unfortunately, many people incorrectly use the word "ego" to suggest an inflated ego, which is entirely different. The ego is simply your perception of yourself, but those with an 'inflated ego' or a 'large ego' have an overinflated sense of self or worth.

In a sales situation where you are rewarded for success, becoming egotistical is possible. Of course, you want to be rewarded for being productive, but be careful not to believe your own hype too much. Enjoy it to a point, but stay focused so that it doesn't impact your ego in a way that prevents you from working hard, going the extra mile, or being selfless.

It's important to show humility in all aspects of your role and your job, as you will learn something different at each stage. ***Humility allows you to improve.*** **However, if you've got an inflated ego,**

you can't work on yourself because you believe you already have it all worked out.

It's key to gain people's trust whilst in the sales process and show the customer that you believe in yourself and your product. Showing an overly inflated ego can be off-putting to the customer, however, because you might make the sales process about you rather than them. There must be a shift in focus from yourself to the client and their problems, and you must explain how you will solve the problem for them, not for yourself.

I've come to realise that being overly familiar with people can be a turnoff, and I learned this the hard way. You know how it is when someone approaches you and invades your personal space with excessive familiarity. It can be uncomfortable, even if the situation is not inherently wrong. That's why I want to emphasise the importance of being measured in conversations and allowing others to respond. It's crucial to dial up enthusiasm at the right moment and dial it back down so that people can absorb what you're sharing without feeling overwhelmed. Reading the room is also essential because you must be aware of how people react and respond to you. I've been in many situations where the conversation was entirely one-sided, and the other person spent the entire time talking about themselves without bothering to ask me any questions. While it's true that people tend to come away from conversations where they talk about themselves feeling more fulfilled, it's important to strike a balance and make a connection rather than just trying to sell something.

Imposter Syndrome

Do you ever feel like you don't deserve the amazing things that have come your way? Maybe you've been promoted, received high accolades, and reached all your KPI's, but you're still telling yourself it was good timing or luck. Despite having the education, experience, and talent to back up your success, you can't shake off the feeling that you're a fraud.

If this sounds familiar, you might be dealing with impostor syndrome. It's not an official diagnosis, but mental health specialists have recognised it for its prevalence and the anxiety, stress, and hopelessness it can cause.

Even though they are intelligent and skilled, people with impostor syndrome always worry that they will be found to be fakes. However, there are a few indicators to look out for, such as perfectionism, pushing yourself to exhaustion, downplaying your successes, being anxious about making mistakes, and brushing off compliments.

But the good news is that you're not alone and can overcome impostor syndrome. By acknowledging your abilities and hard work, accepting compliments, and practising self-compassion, you can build your confidence and start to believe in your success.

Imposter syndrome is a biggie when it comes to Sales Confidence, and believe it or not, it predominantly affects high achievers. Imposter syndrome impacts my anxiety and depression, because it makes me doubt my achievements, abilities, forget all of my valid experiences, the positive outcomes and successes in my career. It may cause me to lose confidence in myself, at which point I turn into 'the imposter'. I can see myself as an inadequate human being who is incapable and a failure. I internalise the notion that I am a fraud, that I shouldn't have what I do, and that Sales Confidence is unjustified. When I experience imposter syndrome, I feel inadequate and enter a state of fight or flight, which makes me want to start removing myself from situations. Have you ever felt any of these emotions? If yes, the good news is that it's normal.

I had a job at LinkedIn, but I was always anxious because I felt like an imposter. I had been chosen for one of the top companies globally, with one of the best cultures of belonging and inclusion, yet, I would automatically avoid sitting next to particularly positive people because I was overwhelmed by their good attitude. I would hide in the office corner, so I didn't have to be near them. That is one example of how imposter syndrome has impacted me.

The issue with COVID most likely exacerbated impostor syndrome for many people, as I believe you need to expose yourself to others in order to overcome that mindset. During Covid, people were protected from having to measure themselves against other people, which is on one hand a good thing, but you should also strive to improve yourself by observing others. Imposter syndrome can often strike when you first start something, and that's okay because you are new to it, and you might feel incompetent. It's when imposter syndrome becomes more extreme that it becomes a problem. When you grow to be overly anxious and depressed, you must begin to counter that by checking how you perceive yourself and noticing how kind (or not) your self-talk is.

Imposter syndrome can, in some circumstances, be a positive motivator at the beginning of a career or the start of a new job. **Another unexpected benefit is that it can help you become more interpersonal, which will, in turn, prevent your ego from over-inflating.** Ultimately, it's likely that at some point most of us will encounter imposter syndrome - the main thing is to notice, acknowledge it, and carry on regardless.

Keep in mind that if you *were* an imposter, you would not be promoted, complemented, trusted, or applauded.

From my own experience, I can't stress enough how crucial it is to work with a therapist or psychologist. A safe space where you can have an unfiltered conversation with someone who is not a friend, colleague, or manager is immensely helpful. I've been able to face my challenges head-on with the help of a professional who is trained to guide me through difficult moments.

But that's just the beginning. Working with a professional coach takes it to the next level. They give you feedback and structure to help you work through your problems and reach your goals. This kind of support is invaluable, especially regarding professional goals.

That's why I'm proud that our Sales Confidence membership offers this type of support. It's not just about sales tactics or closing deals but about taking care of yourself as a whole person. With the help of a therapist or coach, you can overcome obstacles and reach new heights in your career and personal life.

Treat imposter syndrome as it is: *an illusion.*

Imposter syndrome is a common struggle that can be challenging to overcome. But the first step is acknowledging that you have it. Don't let embarrassment or guilt prevent you from opening up to someone you trust, such as a friend, partner, or therapist. Sharing your low self-esteem is an essential step toward overcoming imposter syndrome. Recognise that it's normal to feel like an outsider in new situations, such as a job change or being the only one from a minority group at your company. It's important to find safe spaces to acknowledge these emotions and not let them make you feel inadequate.

When things don't go as planned, try accepting the lesson, giving yourself some compassion, and moving on. Remember that mistakes are okay, and you're entitled to bad days like anyone else.

If you're a perfectionist, focus on excelling where it counts the most and letting go of the small stuff. Instead, dedicate some time to yourself, and find out what you need to do to care for yourself.

Finally, try imagining yourself succeeding. Define your success in specific terms and picture yourself successfully navigating a challenging scenario. Putting your plans into words gives you a better chance of seeing them come to fruition.

Remember, you're not alone; with dedication, you can overcome imposter syndrome.

PILLAR TWO

WELLBEING

CHAPTER SIX
MIND, BODY & CONFIDENCE

Mindfulness

Implementing mindfulness into your business and your life.

MINDFULNESS, to me, is an exercise in pausing, breathing, being present, and not being anxious or concerned about what lies ahead. It takes a bit of time out of your day to centre yourself, be present, and pause.

Taking time to reflect and be present before entering a conversation is critical to centering yourself. When you're nervous about going into a situation, you start to escalate your thinking so remember to take a moment before the situation to breathe, centre yourself, compose yourself, and be present. If you prepare yourself this way, you are less likely to be swept up in any anxiety about the situation, and you will feel more grounded. Then, once you've centred and given yourself some capacity to breathe, you can start thinking about what you've got ahead of you.

Three Tips for Mindfulness

1. Do your best to find somewhere quiet, and turn off all notifications and distractions. Make sure

you give yourself enough time to fully unplug. You don't need to take more than five minutes, but I try to take at *least* five minutes to become still, pause and be without distraction.

2. Be aware, but don't judge the unconscious trail of thought going on in your mind. Just watch it and let it pass. Your mind will be talking to you regardless of whether you're trying to be at peace, but let it flow.

3. Centre yourself. You can do this by quietly naming things in your head. For example, name something you can see, something you can feel, something you can smell or taste, and something you can hear. By grounding yourself in the present moment, you are less likely to feel anxiety moving into the next moment.

Body

Being a salesperson is like being an elite athlete (I hear you laughing but hear me out on this!). It's like being an athlete because so much is involved in the upkeep, as you need to tend to both your emotional and physical well-being to be at the top of your game. To be a high achiever, you need to have a healthy body. From a nutritional perspective, you should be mindful about eating healthily, and eating at reasonable times. It's also essential to exercise daily, even if that means simply going out for a walk for 30 minutes. I think more than ever people need to invest in structured time for exercise as we've all reduced our daily steps because of the lack of movement in office work and especially from working from home. Often, we move from our bedroom to our kitchen and our desk only. That reduces the activity in our daily lives and will ultimately make us unhealthy and unable to perform at our best. Anything that raises your heartbeat will increase those positive endorphins, helping you maintain a peak body and, therefore, peak mindset. Body and mindset are intertwined and must be looked after effectively.

I train in the gym about five times a week, with a mixture of cardiovascular exercise and weights. I enjoy running and using the rowing machine, but I also do body weights, from squats to deadlifts and bench presses. My routine allows me to get away from the stresses of work and focus on myself. Enhancing my body and becoming stronger makes my mind healthier, which helps my productivity from a success perspective.

Even if you aren't naturally active, you should think about getting up from your desk more often and be careful about being stationary too long. If you find that difficult, you can schedule when you need to get up and move around by setting an alarm on your phone.

I work in 'time blocks'. A time block could be a 90-minute time block of productivity before you have a break. If you can create a plan in your diary that schedules you to go for a walk or get up from your desk, you will start to notice how little you were doing it before (and how good you feel once you start!).

For others, bodywork might be low-impact exercises like yoga or pilates. I would advise trying several different exercise options and seeing what works best for you. If you don't like gyms, or you work from home and have children, hundreds of thousands of free videos are available to suit any person or workout situation. Even if working out is new to you, I stress that you should begin with some movement each day and see how it radically changes your life.

Confidence

What is confidence when it comes to well-being? I believe that if you think you're healthy, acknowledge that you're strong, and believe that you can push your body further than you are used to, you will begin to grow in confidence in ALL areas of your life. All that positive muscle memory and all with help to push yourself in your day-to-day role and will give you confidence in overcoming the challenges and the objections you face every day as a salesperson. As a salesperson, you're getting rejected every day, pushback, and being told "no", which can create pressure, stress, and anxiety. However, you will learn to cope much more easily with these challenges if your well-being is taken care of. Again, if you *believe* that you are well, you act as though you *are* well, and you will come across as a positive human being, enhancing your mood and that of other people, creating a feel-good factor. If you feel good in yourself, you'll help others feel good about what you're selling. If you don't feel good about yourself as regards your well-being, that will come across to your colleagues and customers. Your well-being will dictate how much energy you've got to allocate throughout your day and how much energy you've got to allocate to forthcoming meetings or customer conversations. So having confidence in your well-being is about having faith in your energy levels so that when you need it, your energy is available to you to deliver the best outcomes.

Obviously, as per the name of my business, confidence is at the core of my brand. As I mentioned at the beginning of the book, it was 2017 when I coined the term 'Sales Confidence'. I wanted the brand to feel positive, and perhaps even look good on a t-shirt! I didn't want it to be a sales 'elite'. I didn't want the brand to be elitist at all, instead I wanted it to be accessible to everybody. That's how I came to 'Sales Confidence' and many people are already adopting the sentiment. Lots of people have come up with their own definitions of what Sales Confidence means to them, which is wonderful – the term is becoming part of the lexicon that people use as a definition of success. For example, "are you Sales Confident or do you have Sales Confidence?" is a question that people ask themselves in interviews or during their day-to-day mindfulness checks. True confidence will often lead to better results.

Sustainable Success

We covered sustainable success earlier in the book, but here are some practical tips towards achieving it. Often, salespeople will drive themselves to burn out early in their careers.

Success must be sustainable, so you can continue onwards and upwards without damaging your mindset or your health.

Here are some tips that can help you achieve your goals while staying healthy and balanced:

1. Set realistic goals: When working in sales, it can be tempting to set aggressive targets that will push you to work harder and close more deals. However, it's essential to make sure your goals are achievable and sustainable in the long term. Setting unrealistic targets can lead to burnout and disappointment, ultimately harming your sales performance.

2. Focus on building relationships: Sales is all about relationships. Rather than just trying to close deals, focus on building genuine connections with your customers. This will not only help you close more deals, but it will also make your work more fulfilling and enjoyable.

3. Stay organised: Sales can be chaotic, with many leads, contacts, and follow-ups to manage. Ensure you have a system in place for keeping track of everything, whether a CRM tool or a simple spreadsheet. Being organised will help you stay on top of your workload and avoid feeling overwhelmed.

4. Take care of your physical and mental health: Sales can be stressful, so taking care of yourself physically and mentally is essential. Ensure you

get enough sleep, eat a healthy diet, and exercise regularly. Consider practising mindfulness or meditation to help manage stress and stay focused.

5. Continuously learn and improve: Successful salespeople are constantly learning and growing. Stay current with industry trends, attend conferences or workshops, and seek feedback from colleagues and customers. You'll be better equipped to succeed in the long term by continuously improving your skills.

Remember, achieving healthy, sustainable success in sales is not a sprint; it's a marathon. By building relationships, staying organised, taking care of your health, and continuously learning, you'll be well on your way to achieving your goals while maintaining a healthy work-life balance.

Wellbeing Team

I believe we should all have a 'wellbeing team'; an inner circle of experts and individuals who know our psyche. I have my own wellbeing team, including a psychologist, a psychiatrist, a personal trainer, a mentor, and a coach. These are individuals that I can pull on throughout the week or month and ask how I'm doing and use that opportunity to speak freely without being judged. So I invest in that team – I pay for a private psychologist, private psychiatrist and a private personal trainer. They're guiding me along my journey to ensure I'm optimising my health and wellbeing. Having a wellbeing team means a group of people are holding you accountable for your wellbeing and success.

Accountability

Of course, not everybody has the financial freedom to build a wellbeing team. Instead, you can find accountability partners that will have a similar effect. You will need to find a peer—or a group of peers—at your level who you can work with to hold each other accountable.

Also, there are mentors out there who don't charge. Usually, you can go to your mentor for anything you need to gain extra insight, so choose wisely. Anyone can be a mentor to you, but I would look for mentors with two to five years' experience ahead of you. Identify the skills and knowledge you don't yet have, and you can lean on them for advice and expertise throughout your journey. In return, you can help them in other ways.

Mentorship

People are often fearful or unknowledgeable about approaching a mentor and thus have trouble gaining one. It doesn't have to be daunting, however. Start with LinkedIn—run a search on LinkedIn and identify people that have got, as I said, three to five years more experience than you. Then you need to message them. Point out that you've identified something interesting in their profile, that you like the look of their experience, that you're looking for a mentor and would love to have a conversation with them to understand if they're willing to share some of their expertise and advice. That is the most effective way to do it. Another way is going out to your network and asking other people if they know someone that could be helpful to you. Your immediate network might not be the potential people you want as mentors, but they might know others with the right experience. Draw up a list of a hundred people, and I can guarantee that if you spoke to all those hundred, you would find the right person.

Therapy

Therapy has been a huge competitive advantage for me because it gives you a safe space. I have talked about safe spaces before, but it's even more effective with an expert who allows you to share all your woes and talk about your hardships without being judged. Workplace-related annoyances might not seem like they are affecting you emotionally, but everything has an emotional impact on us. It's helpful to have a therapist who can guide us, give us positive, reaffirming feedback, and let us talk freely without judging us. I would recommend therapy to everybody because it's a unique environment where you can say anything, and you will not be judged for it. Whereas if you seek guidance from people who aren't professionals in therapy, you might find they have too much baggage and history associated with the topic and want to influence you in a certain way. **A therapist lets you be and bring your entire self to the environment, enables you to speak to your inner child and allows that inner child to express themselves comfortably.** This means that any challenges or upsets that rise to the surface can be acknowledged without you feeling uncomfortable about them.

Of course, finances can mean that therapy appears off limits to many. Still, you'd be surprised to learn that therapy can be pretty cheap these days, especially with online therapists, et cetera. There is also free therapy, but there is often a waiting list. Many starting out in their careers might not have the financial freedom to gain immediate therapy. To that, I would say that if you're looking to become employed, you should look for companies investing in those services. A lot of companies provide employee assistance programs or additional wellbeing services. I think it's a good measure of a company if they're invested in the wellbeing of their staff. That should measure what you are looking at when you're looking for companies.

Nutrition

Did you know that what you eat can significantly impact your confidence and performance? Eating a healthy, well-balanced diet can give you the energy and focus you need to be at your best daily. When you fuel your body with the proper nutrients, you'll have more power throughout the day, which can help you stay alert and focused during sales calls and meetings.

In addition, eating healthy can also help you feel more confident in your role. When you care for your body, you send a message to yourself and others that you value your health and well-being. This can translate to increased confidence and a more positive attitude, which as we know is incredibly beneficial in sales.

So, what should you be eating to support your performance in a sales role? Aim for a balanced diet with plenty of fresh fruits and vegetables, lean protein sources like chicken and fish, whole grains, and healthy fats like avocado and nuts, and remember to stay hydrated by drinking plenty of water throughout the day!

By prioritising your nutrition and caring for your body, you'll set yourself up for success in your sales career. So, fuel up with some healthy, nutritious foods—your body (and your career!) will thank you for it.

I find it imperative to be aware of what I put into my body and understand what energy is gained or suppressed from what I consume. It's not always about avoiding anything, there are times in the day when I need a sugar rush, mornings when I'm thinking about lunch already, and days when I think, "I need to be moving a lot today". I might decide that I want a bit of a sugar rush, but I also must be aware of the impact that what I'm putting in my body is going to have. For example, if I've got an important meeting in the afternoon, I may not have such a large lunch. A large lunch will suppress my feelings, dampen my energy levels, and make me tired.

We must be aware that what we consume affects our energy levels. Think about being sustained throughout the day—are you missing breakfast or having too large a breakfast? Are you having a heavy lunch causing you to slump too much in the afternoon? If so, that's a natural part of your digestive system, and you shouldn't this book your most important meetings in the afternoon. Next, think about snacking. How do you snack throughout the day? Do you nibble on chocolate bars or crisps or chew on nuts and fruit? No judgement on yourself, but become aware of your eating habits, as so many of our habits are subconscious.

I've recently started to use a company called Gusto. They make home delivery boxes, which are meals that you cook yourself but are prepared. They are not takeaway or ready-made meals, but they come in an organised way, which helps me control my calorie intake and what I'm putting into my body. One of the challenges I have with having three children is that there are a lot of bad snacks around that I have to do my best to avoid. Having the self-discipline not to eat the crisps or snacks in front of me and choosing to eat the fruit, salad or nuts is a small battle that I fight every day. The good news is that I am now conscious of it, whereas, before, I wasn't. Of course, as with anything, good nutrition takes baby steps, but just making small adjustments here and there.

Route Out of Sales

I think it's fair to say at some point in your career, you might discover that sales simply isn't the career for you, and you may have sought this book because you're lacking confidence and success in sales. It's okay to realise that sales is not for you, and you would like to find a different route into another career. There are a lot of areas you can go into once you have developed sales skills. In addition, sales skills will often put you in a stronger position when it comes to hiring.

Realising that sales isn't for you isn't a failure. Perhaps you can't cope with the monthly targets, the back and forth, the rejection, and the stress that comes with that. Despite taking all the guidance from the available books, sales may not suit you as a career. If you're feeling that way, it's worthwhile thinking about what else you could be doing.

I wanted to leave a message here. It's okay not to be okay. It's okay to discover that sales isn't for you and want to move away from it. If you're reading this book thinking, "do you know what—this is too much. This isn't for me"—that's all good - awareness is critical. There are plenty of other possible business routes for you to follow.

Make a list of your interests and what excites you in a potential career move. We only get one shot at this life, so if sales is getting you down, don't worry that you have wasted time; you have a considerable head start in your future career with the transferable skill set.

CHAPTER SEVEN

MEASURING YOURSELF AGAINST YOURSELF

WE LIVE in a LinkedIn, Instagram, Facebook and TikTok-preoccupied world and are thus constantly comparing ourselves to people we don't know. We see a virtual story they want to put out in the world rather than actually who that person is. We don't know exactly what they do, what they're good at, what they're not good at, what their limitations are, what their failures are, what their worries are, and what their insecurities are. We don't know any of that on the whole. Yet we compare ourselves to other people when really, the only person you should compare yourself to is the person you were last week, last year, five years ago or ten years ago. Only worry about how much you have improved as an individual.

Monitor your progress by comparing yourself against targets you set for yourself and not those of other people. For example, measure yourself against the person you were yesterday.

I reflect on this often. A small example is that I'm doing five sessions of exercise weekly, which I wasn't doing before Christmas. One of the things I've started doing is running in the mornings before work. I used to do that successfully in the past but had a period last year where I was somewhat depressed, and I didn't want to exercise, against my own good advice. However, if you look at them compared to what I'm doing now, I'm proud of myself. I'm proud that I got myself through that depressive episode and that I'm on my feet and working on a new business. However, then I log onto LinkedIn, and I see people that have similar businesses to me, and they've been doing it for five years, and I start to think that I should have the same success as them, and it begins to eat away at me. I remember to only value what I'm gaining and how I'm developing myself, rather than comparing myself to others.

Spiritual

Thinking about your spirituality above material things will help you always keep your feet on the ground. Being mindful about how you relate to something is more important than the things that you are looking to gain. It affects how you see yourself instead of how you interact with material things and the things happening around you. You're more likely to be centred and happy if you focus on the spiritual aspects of your life than your material things outside of yourself. You can't necessarily change what's happening when you gain material things, but you can change how you relate to those material things once you've achieved them.

Love and Friendship

Sales is about relationships. So, if you seek out friendships in your career, you are in a great position to develop good relationships. Bring love to the table, and care about the outcomes. You're persuading people to go down and express a loving perspective rather than a hunter mentality, 'seek to kill'. So often in sales, they talk about having a 'hunter mentality, which is seeking out businesses, but it's not a great phrase, as what do hunters do? They kill animals. That's not love; that's not a sign of friendship and not rewarding. Whereas if you can seek to solve someone's problems and genuinely change their life and business, you'll find a lot of love in those scenarios.

This is the positive mindset approach you should take in your sales process. Not many people will talk about this, as maybe it's a little bit to the left, but I feel that if you treat people as you want to be treated, they will respect you, and you're going to develop a friendship. That leads to a form of love—not in the sense of 'being in love—but in a sense ", I love working with this person because they make me feel good. They solve my problems, and they help me achieve my goals".

If you can do those three things, you can keep a great relationship with someone, which is a huge positive that stays with you in your career and life. I'm now very close friends with several people I've sold to, and I can't think of a better indication of the relationships I've created than maintaining long-term friendships due to a sale.

Remember to Have Fun

Without a doubt, this element is crucial! If you're not having a good time, you need to reflect on what you're doing. If you're being successful yet burning yourself out, it's not sustainable and won't be fun. If you're making money, but you're having a hard time with your boss week in and week out, that's not fun. It's essential to try and have a good time because it comes across how you express yourself with the people you're interacting with. There should be an element of fun in every stage of the sales process, so you must find out what parts are fun so that you can double down on them.

Thai culture has a word, 'sanook', which means finding fun in every endeavour. In the spirit of sanook, the Thai people try to find joy in everything they do, whether work or pleasure and in every action. I believe the west could learn a lot from that mindset. There are so many mundane aspects in the prospecting role of a salesperson—which is when they have to do their outreach—but if you can find fun in changing a few words in your emails, or you can see the fun side of someone telling you to "piss off", you can even embrace the rejection. Try and find the fun in making someone successful and happy. That way, you will have a better time and be more successful. So fun and confidence are essential to making sure you make the most of your day and week.

Developing Your System

A system is a group of parts that are connected and always work together to get the same result. In your daily life, having effective systems in place is crucial for being productive throughout the day, and to make these systems, you need to think about their structure, how useful they will be, and the tasks they will require. For example, when you talk to someone, you need a plan to determine their needs, which is called the discovery conversation.

To achieve an effective outcome, you need to have several systems working together seamlessly, and developing a sense of intertwining and integrating these systems is vital to becoming a successful salesperson. Without efficient systems in place, it's difficult to achieve sustainable success.

The various systems necessary for success can be categorised into task-based, emotional, and framework systems. Task-based systems focus on the practical aspects of completing a task or achieving a goal, and emotional systems are centred around managing and controlling emotions to remain focused on the task at hand. Framework systems help you decide what to do and make sure that all the parts of the system work well together.

PILLAR THREE

PERFORMANCE

CHAPTER EIGHT
GETTING AHEAD AS A NEW SALESPERSON

Where New Salespeople Go Wrong

Not Listening

THERE'S A LONG LIST of ways new salespeople typically go wrong, but rule number one—you must listen to discover what the client needs before you can sell them anything. First and foremost, many new salespeople don't listen and talk too much; that's the most common onearea. Usually, the salesperson may be on the phone, Zoom or Microsoft Teams or whatever it might be, and they're excited about the product and the company they work for. They're excited to be there and have the conversation, and that's all great, but more often than not, new salespeople end up using their mouths way too much rather than using two ears and one mouth. Then, the ratio is off, and they end up talking at the person rather than asking them thoughtful questions and listening. Talking and not listening is the most significant and primary way new salespeople can fail.

Not Pain Solving

Another area is being too focused on the product and its features and not problem-solving for the customer. They are forcing the feature without matching a problem to their feature, which is not problem-solving. Every customer is looking to either move away from pain or move towards pleasure. Most likely, however, a customer is looking to solve a pain. Unless you ask the right questions and then focus on the problems that your product can solve, you will miss the opportunity to persuade them to go with your solution. Your solution must solve their pain; feature bashing is not going to get the sale.

Feature Bashing

When you begin a new role, you tend to find yourself in a position where you are filling your mind with new information about a product and a service, and you're excited about all the features. This might lead you to listing features without listening - this is feature bashing. If you don't spend enough time understanding what your product solves for the prospect and the problem that it solves, you're unlikely to make a sale.

Anybody can fall into the feature bashing trap, but it's more of a problem with new salespeople because they don't appreciate how much they need to engage with their prospects and listen to understand their concerns and needs.

Price over Value

Another area new salespeople go wrong is focusing on price over than value. Structuring a deal around the price rather than the value will not get sales.

Not Closing

This one may sound obvious, but you've got to ask for the sale. I'll say it again—ask for the business! Many people do their whole pitch and go through the entire process but forget to ask for the sale. You must remember to close. (Close close close!)

Lack of Research

New salespeople who present a lack of research or a lack of discovery about who they're interacting with will likely fall at the first hurdle. There are many tools available today to find this information, so there are few excuses. There are company websites, news sites, LinkedIn, and social media channels about an individual. You can easily look up most people on Instagram or Twitter and find many things about them. You can and should utilise these tools to set you up for success and help you prepare; if you don't prepare, you will miss a considerable trick and will across as someone they shouldn't be doing business with. If you appear unprepared, you will likely miss out on an opportunity.

Interviewing

Interviewing is a critical element of presenting yourself in the best light to make you attractive to a hiring manager. You've got to build trust and rapport with a hiring manager to position yourself as a top candidate. There are many things that need to be considered during interview, such as presentation. These days of course, many interviews are online, in which case, there are many points to check. Have you got a clear background? Have you got good lighting? Do you immediately smile when you greet someone and show your teeth? (I personally believe that is very important). How much energy are you putting into the screen? Remember, you're in 2D and you're not in front of the interviewer. Still, they need to feel your energy from the volume and tone of your voice and how you emphasise your key points with your words.

Research the company

Spend a few hours learning everything you can about the company—from as many sources as possible. Talk to people in your network to find current and previous employees, read recent news releases, and spend some time on Google. So often, candidates look at the information a company is pushing out on its website and social media accounts but fail to look more closely at what others say. By looking at multiple sources, you'll get a broader picture of the company (along with any negative press) and be ready to talk about why you'd like to work there and what you can do for them.

Learn everything you can about the position.

Before you show your interviewer why you'd be a great fit, you need to know what they're looking for. Luckily, most organisations have outlined exactly what they want in a job posting. So go back to the description you looked at before you applied. What skills and experiences are they emphasising? What problems will this hire need to solve? These are the things you'll want to highlight throughout your interview. Some, however, will not have outlined the job as well. In that case, either speak to the recruiter or call the hiring manager beforehand to get this information. This action will also make you appear proactive.

Try out the company's product/service where possible.

If the company you're interviewing for sells a product you can feasibly check out—try it before your interview. If hired, your goal will be to create value for those who use that product, and being a user, yourself is the first step. Plus, it'll help show the hiring manager that you're genuinely interested in the role.

Learn about the interviewers

If you're not told who you'll meet with during your interview, ask! For each interviewer, learn what their role at the company is and prep some questions that are specific to them. For example, you can ask for details about their role, discuss current events related to their field, or bring up a common interest you know outside the office (stick to one mentioned in an easily accessible spot, like their company bio or LinkedIn profile).

Find out what kind of interview you're in for—and prepare accordingly.

Companies use different types of interviews, so ask what you'll be faced with. For example, some companies will have you meet one-on-one with several different people at the company. In contrast, others might have you meet with multiple people at once or give an interview presentation. You may also have a phone or video interview. Asking the recruiter or HR contact about the interview format ahead of time is fair game. And once you know, investing time to become familiar with this style can make a huge difference.

Brush up on interview skills and common interview questions

Next, you'll want to use what you learned to prepare your answers to common interview questions and practise some interview techniques.

Identify your selling points for this job

Even if you're an interviewing megastar, it's essential to spend time thinking carefully about what skills, accomplishments, and interview answers will resonate with your interviewers most for this job. Your management abilities? Your creativity? Go back to your research and see what makes you most qualified.

Tell the interviewer about yourself.

For every interview, you'll want an answer to "Tell me about yourself" tailored to this job and company and ready to go. Interviewers almost always ask this question or a similar one—like "Walk me through your resume"—to start the conversation, so you want to ensure you're getting started on the right foot.

Know why you're interested in this position at this company

You'll likely get asked why you're interested in this particular role and company. Make sure you can answer, identify critical factors about the job and the organisationorganisation that align well with your strengths, interests, and work style and get you excited about the position. Even if you're not asked about this, you can use this to inform your answers to other questions.

Do some salary research

Even if you're not ready to have the money conversation, you might still get asked about your salary expectations. So to keep yourself from getting caught off guard and giving (or agreeing to) a way-too-low number, do some salary research to figure out how you'd answer.

Tap into your memory

Most interviewers will ask at least a few behavioural questions to get an idea of how you've acted or would act in specific scenarios. While you can't anticipate every possible situation you'll be asked about; you can prepare a few stories about your past work experiences that you can adapt as needed.

The STAR method.

When answering interview questions with a story, you want to ensure that the story is well-structured and the takeaway is clear. Your goal should be to give your interviewer all the context they need to understand what happened while still answering the question clearly and concisely. One way to do this is by using the STAR method. STAR stands for:

Situation: Briefly describe the scenario in enough detail so the interviewer will understand the stakes and everything else in your answer.

Task: Talk about what your role in the situation was.

Action: Discuss what you did and why.

Result: Tell your interviewer about the outcome and what you learned.

You might want to tweak this structure slightly for some questions. For example, if you're talking about a time you demonstrated leadership skills, consider defining what leadership means to you before jumping into the situation. But the STAR method will ensure your stories always have a beginning, middle, and end.

Write down essential numbers and details.

Find some revenue figures, engagement numbers, budget or team sizes, percentages of time saved, or anything else you have achieved to communicate your impact.

Brush up on your interview skills.

How well you answer interview questions isn't everything—though it is a lot. Interviewers are also consciously or subconsciously picking up on how well you use other interview skills, such as active listening, small talk, and empathy. These skills not only help impress an interviewer but also give them a sense of what it might be like to work with you as a colleague.

***Practise* your answers to common interview questions.**

You can and should familiarise yourself with common interview questions—but don't prepare by writing out your entire answer; instead, jot down a few notes or bullet points. Practice looking in the mirror and answering them out loud. This prep work will help clarify your thoughts and make you much more comfortable during the interview.

Body language

Brush up on what specific body language conveys. Be aware of what you're communicating through your posture and stance—and make sure it's good. (For example, sitting with your arms and legs crossed sends a message that you are closed-off or feel defensive.) Think your movements through ahead of time, so you're not distracted (or distracting) during the interview. If you're on video, think about how you'll show that you're actively engaged in that format—putting the Zoom window near your camera, so you're not looking away from your interviewer, for example, or making non-verbal gestures or expressions to show that you're listening without cutting off their microphone.

Try some mock interviews.

If you have the time, do a few mock interviews with somebody you trust. Then, you'll be much better at answering, "What would you bring to the position?" the 100th time you do it, and you'll know how to sit comfortably ahead of time.

Questions that you will ask

Most interviews will wrap up with "Do you have any questions for me?" and the answer should always be yes! You should plan some questions that are very specific to the job and company.

Plan what you'll do if asked something you didn't prepare for

How do you prepare for the interview question you weren't expecting? You can develop a go-to phrase to help you avoid tumbleweed if you need time to stall and gather your thoughts. Two strategies that work well are repeating the question thoughtfully before answering or saying, "That is a great question. But, I would have to say...".

Hand movements are also extremely important. You don't want to be flailing your hands everywhere, but you do want to use your hands for emphasis and to highlight the points that you are making. So, it's a three pronged attack—presentation, preparation, and positioning yourself, and *then* it's the story. You must be able to tell a story that will grab the interest of the hiring manager so that they can relate to something about you. This is different from a story you might tell from your experiences. Instead, it should be a form of story that highlights your experience that stands out, and is fun and interesting that will build the interest of the hiring manager. Interested enough so they will be ensured that you are someone they should be talking to.

Preparation

You must always be prepared before going into an interview. That's obvious you should have done your research about the interviewer using LinkedIn understood the person, the individual and the company that they work for.

CV Writing

This is the first impression a company will have of you, and the great news is that it's an art that you can learn to do really well! It's hard to get across everything you are and you have done on one piece of paper, right? People make so many mistakes with their CV's such as having too many pages, and writing long paragraphs – it's like verbal diarrhoea on some CV's with too many words, not specifically highlighting top performance or experience. Especially from a sales perspective, you must include your sales numbers. You must highlight your actual performance against your target, and specify the customers that you've brought on and the activities you were doing. Activities would include, how many calls per day per week, and how many meetings were you booking, what methodologies you've been taught or training you've had.

Don't forget to include major achievements that stand out. Did you make the high achievers club? Presidents club? Salesperson of the month/year? These are elements that must highlight be highlighted on your CV.

Don't lie! This is another major factor. Companies these days, especially tech companies, investigate the profile of experience. So if you didn't go to university, don't make it up. Don't pretend or make up your figures. If you had a bad year, had to take time out for whatever reason, and have a gap in your CV, be honest and explain that gap. It's much more sensible than trying to cover it up or lie.

A one page CV is adequate for most roles.

Most hiring managers are interested in the most recent job you've had, and maybe the one before that. The ones previous, they will be less interested in, especially as that could be five to ten years ago. I tend to find with junior CVs that they will tell you about all the supermarket and bar jobs. No-one cares, we know what working in the bar is; you don't need to go into five paragraphs about what you did in the bar. It's great that you had a job while you were at university - it's a positive, but you don't need to go to the eighth degree explaining it.

Pick a Winning SAAS Company

SAAS means Software as a Service. It's a business model that all the companies I am associated with work with. They're software companies, but they're called SAAS companies because they have a subscription model where the revenue is, what they call, 'recurring'. I not a one-off payment, it's an annual monthly recurring payment, which is the business model of SAAS. Picking a winning company is quite difficult, but really important as you're gambling on your career. You're placing a bet to pick a winner because if you've got the right product, the right people in the organisation, and the right profile of a manager, then headed towards success. You need to assess the company from the outside based on its product, its positioning in the market and its total addressable market.

You must also ask what is the commission structure and what are the accelerators before you go into a role. What will they be supplementing your pay within terms of share options and company bonuses?

Identify what stage of growth they're at. In SAAS, we talk about A, B, C, D, E, F, and G, which are the different funding stages. And if you choose an early stage, which is really early—known as a seed or series A—it's a lot more chaotic, less predictable, less defined in terms of processes and procedures and a higher risk associated with it. But of course, sometimes, with a higher risk comes a higher reward if you become a successful seller in that company. Later stage companies usually have more robust sales processes in place, better training, better sales enablement, and better leaders. Also, there are more examples of salespeople that are already making money.

Then you've got post IPO. So once a company's listed, you can get what's known as RSU—restricted stock option units. These are dependent on the performance of the company on the stock exchange, the New York stock exchange or wherever that company's listed and that can give you extra bonus points and money along the way. You have to look at the market and consider all these different factors, which comes down to the product.

Think about the people that you're going to be associated with, such as the hiring manager, and especially the manager that you will be working for. They say that people don't leave jobs, they leave managers and I totally agree with that. Your manager is absolutely critical to your success and so is their manager as well.

Then you've got the product. Ask, is the product going to be easily understood by your buyers? Does it solve a major problem? Does it provide the buyers a return investment? What stage is the company at? Do they offer other bonuses and extras that you can get excited about? All of these questions are important as you need to go in and understand if the company's going to tick those boxes for you.

Personal Elevator Pitch

You need a 30-second elevator pitch that explains who you are, what you do, what you're great at and why someone should listen to you. And, not to make it sound difficult, but it must come across in a positive, authentic, and enthusiastic way so that people immediately appreciate what you are about. So, for example, my elevator pitch would be: "My name's James Ski. I'm the Founder of Sales Confidence. Sales Confidence is building the world's most valuable B2B sales community, and our mission is to help salespeople at each stage of their career with their mindset, well-being, and performance".

It must be concise to the point that it conveys what value you're looking to provide to the industry. For example, mine highlighted my mission statement and described my overall vision. You can hook them into you as an individual by giving them all that information in less than 30 seconds.

The elevator pitch might sound simple, but it is easy to fluster when under pressure. So prepare your pitch in advance.

You should keep some details of your life private, from your earliest childhood memory to your recent obsession with learning the drums. Instead, this question is created to gain an overview of your work background and why you want to work for them.

Think about your top five experiences at work. Next, consider the personality traits, themes and skills that come across through these experiences. Finally, pick one or two experiences and themes that match the selection criteria for the job and focus on them throughout.

Generally, spend 75% of the pitch briefly explaining your work history, highlighting top experiences, themes and skills. Then, round up your pitch by explaining why you want to work for the employer and give some career goals you could achieve through the position.

Practise **your pitch**

Get a second opinion. A friend or partner can point out any nervous habits, odd phrases, or achievements you've missed.

Strike a balance between ensuring you're well-practised and keeping it sounding natural. Being looser means you can use ad-lib, should the occasion need it.

Top pitching tips:

Keep it short.

Keep it natural: remember to breathe, smile and be yourself.

Avoid jokes: your pitch should echo your professionalism.

Practice: practice makes perfect.

Maintain eye contact: this will make you seem confident. If you are on a video platform, ensure you know where the web camera is and that you are talking to it!

Adapt it for different audiences and experiences: tailor it for maximum effect.

CHAPTER NINE

YOUR CAREER

Each Stage of Your Career

AT EACH STEP of your career you must map it out. You've made a decision to interview, you've profiled that company to decide if it's a winning company, and then you need to think about your transition within that company. So if you're starting out, as what's known as a sales development rep or an SDR, this is the most junior role in an organisation, but one of the most critical, because you are making lots of cold calls. You're banging down the doors and you're opening up conversations for your company to then pass on to what they call the account executive. So then they pass it onto the salesperson, and that's who is actually going to close the deal. Now you have to think about what stage you should be getting your promotion, or you should be asking for a promotion. The skills that you learn as an SDR are absolutely critical throughout your career. There is an impatience of people starting in their career to get promoted quickly. Whereas I suggest that you should be as an SDR for a minimum of 18 to 24 months, then you start thinking about the transition about where you go next and what will be your next stage. It's always good to give a company at least three years.

Again, these are guides and there are lots of variables about why your role and your place in a company can break down. In my recruitment business I'm spending time speaking to people all the time, that are given me information at the interview stage, with changing leadership, or an acquisition happens, or not hitting target, or losing a territory. There's lots of reasons why people decide that a company isn't right for them anymore, and you should always be aware of what's going on in the marketplace so that you can make that right transition and then use that reference to pick a company again. You need to be reassessing all the way along in your career.

30, 60, 90 Day Plan

The 30-60-90-day plan is a three-month strategy for training new sales team members or selling in new markets. The document clearly outlines everything salespeople need to do in order to become comfortable with their new companies or regions and increase their productivity. Having a solid 30-60-90 day sales plan is much more likely to help your business maximise new territories, managers, and reps.

Taking the time to create a three-month plan is also a good means of demonstrating your sales knowledge and standing out from other candidates in your interview for a new position. A realistic picture of a new hire or territory is also provided to managers and reps.

30-60-90 day sales plan outline

The format of a 30-day plan can vary from person to person. The version you create can be tailored to fit your needs. The basic concept is that each 30-day chunk represents a new area of focus: learning, implementing, and improving.

These are the activities and what actions we're going to take in those first 30, 60, and 90 days. You will need to put in a framework, like a workbook or guide to highlight the activities and the goals that you should be setting in those first 30, 60, and 90 days. It's all about setting goals and objectives and the outcomes that you are working towards. This is where you can be building a process so that you can track your own progress against your goals, and also highlight to individuals in the business what you are going to do to ramp up. They will talk about this in your onboarding time, which is the time it takes on board in your role and ramp times—you want to reduce the ramp. It's the time it takes you to get to target.

There's a whole set of activities that you need to be working through, like getting to know and building relationships across the business, and building your territory. The territory plan is preparing a list of companies that you're going to be targeting, and building your sequences in your email. It's your outreach product, so that you've got the right communications going out, crafting your script for your pitch in person and the pitch to people over the phone. It's setting out how many dials you're going to make each day, how many conversations you will have and how many meetings you want to book. There's a whole layer of mathematics that you need to apply to give yourself a fast start; it's really important in those first 90 days.

Your Inner Circle

This is the group of people that you associate with in your career. Imagine like yourself in the middle and then there are other rings of people that are around you – there is your immediate team of people. Often you have what is called a 'solutions engineer'. That is a technical person that helps you sell your product. You have a customer success manager whose job it is to make the customer successful. Then there is the account executive, and an SDR a sales development rep, and of course your manager. There are people that are allocated and aligned to you, but then you need to think further afield. You must look across the business and identify other individuals that you could be useful to you from a mentorship angle that could add value to you and guide you as you navigate your new career. So look at where you are in the business and identify a top performer to work with. Always look for individuals that can give you guidance and mentorship. I like to find someone in product, who will give feedback. Understanding what the product roadmap is and getting close to a product person will help you understand the product better. Then you should also be accessing the current customers, identifying customers that you can call on and identifying the persona of the individual. That way you can understand what problems you're solving, what problems your product solves for individuals and how much value your product adds to an individual. Once you start to draw this out, you'll find you have individuals around you whom you can draw on for expertise and guidance outside the immediate people you are allocated to. It means looking beyond and keeping your head up. You should be giving value back to people in the business as much as you are taking as well. Building a tight inner circle of people whose expertise your can draw on to accelerate your learning is essential. We are an accumulation of the main seven people that you surround yourself by, so choosing them well is imperative

Activity, Activity, Activity

You can never escape the fact that sales is a numbers game. How you work and deliver that activity from a mathematical perspective is essential. If your target is £1,000,000 a year and you break that down to 80K a month, then you've got to then break that down to a week, which means breaking down the deals and calculating what activities you need to do to get a meeting. How many emails will you need to send to get that meeting? How many phone calls will it take? Imagine it like a maths equation or a formula to how you work out how you're going to hit your target. Then you need to follow that formula daily. What you put in at the top will impact how much it comes out at the bottom of the funnel. Make sure you are running at maximum activity and follow that activity habitually. That number of activities each day is critical.

The Advantages of Employing an Activity-Based Marketing Method

You only have so much influence over the situation when you're a salesperson. You do not have any influence over the quantity of accessible funds that your customer has. You do not influence whether or not a rival is pursuing the same potential customer as you are. However, sales activities are something that both you and your sales staff can control. You and your team control the number of calls you make. You have complete command over the number of emails you send out. You have absolute power over the number of appointments you schedule. And each of these things - each of these actions - contribute to achieving the revenue goals and business objectives you want.

You and your team need to keep your attention fixed on the endeavours that will bring success for your company to achieve its objectives. But how can you ensure that the things you choose to concentrate on are appropriate? Data!

Monitoring of Sales Activity as Part of Management

Keeping up with the data requires keeping track of activities. Tracking activities is an essential part of managing sales since it lets you see what your team is up to daily and provides data that you can analyse to determine which sales activities are most productive.

Suppose your team is having difficulties meeting the quarterly revenue objectives that you've set for them, but you don't honestly know what they're doing daily. How can you possibly expect to identify the problem and address it? First, you must be aware of the tasks your team is doing and the frequency with which they are carrying them out.

The next step is to compare the members of the team who have the highest performance to those who have the lowest performance and see which members of the team are regularly reaching their quarterly targets. The distinction in the activity level between the two groups is where you will discover the answer to achieving your objectives.

There are many particular ways in which activities tracking might be beneficial to your company, including the following:

- Assists sales managers in locating issues and making necessary course adjustments in real time
- It offers an understanding of the actions that exceptional achievers take that ultimately result in their success.
- It emphasises items that sales representatives are in charge of and can directly impact.

Identify Issues and Make Real-Time Adjustments to Your Strategy

Monitoring activity allows you to identify the source of any performance issues that may arise. You can determine where the problem is coming from by looking at your team's activities if you see that they are not on track to reach their goals.

Instead of waiting until the end of the month or quarter to discover that your team will not meet its revenue objectives, you will be able to make course corrections sooner should difficulties occur. In addition, you'll have a clear idea of what to train your representatives on, and you'll be able to see how much progress they make throughout your instruction.

Acquire an understanding of the actions actually work

It's not hard to figure out which activities lead to success if you compare the routines of your best performers to those of your worst performers and look for similarities and differences. In addition, after the underachievers have been identified, you may teach them how to improve their performance in successful activities.

Use the data collected from your activities to determine the best performers in each step of your sales process and pay attention to the exact behaviours they exhibit for each and find out what they are doing differently from the rest of your representatives.

You will now be able to design a coaching approach for any members of your team who are not top achievers now that you have these insights. Convert the methods that have proven successful for some team members into standardised procedures that the rest of the group can follow.

Pay Attention to the Things That Sales Representatives Can Control

Monitoring your sales efforts provides a road map that will lead you to achieve your goals.

You'll be able to get your team to focus on what they can do once you've figured out what activities make certain team members successful and which give them trouble. So, for example, instead of giving your sales representatives general instructions to 'attract new clients,' you should advise them on the actions that you have found to be most effective in bringing in new consumers.

Give your sales agents clear direction on acquiring more clients by applying the information you've obtained from tracking the behaviours of high performers compared to those of low performers. Then, focus on the tasks that will help you get new clients, starting with the most basic step of figuring out how many calls or meetings you need to set up.

Not only will it benefit your current staff, but identifying successful activities will also assist new sales reps in getting up to speed more quickly. Representatives are aware of what they need to do to achieve their goals by the time they've reached the point where they're fully ramped, and managers are aware of which behaviours to train reps on as they advance in their careers.

The Amount of Money Obtained as a Result of Various Sales Activities

Effective sales leaders grasp the cause-and-effect link between sales efforts and revenue and the fact that the former is a direct outcome of the latter. This comprehension serves as the basis for activity-based selling, which entails supervising sales representatives based on the actions that result in sales.

This method is successful because it focuses on leading indicators and metrics over which a sales team directly control, such as the number of calls made, emails received, meetings booked, etc. You and your team can make modifications in real time with the help of these leading indicators, which will guarantee that you are on the correct route to achieve your goals in the future.

CHAPTER TEN
FUNDAMENTALS

Cold Calling

A GOOD LAYOUT and structure of a cold call will give you the best hope of making it successful. The art of the cold call is having a script and breaking down a call to understand that you've got less than 10 seconds to capture someone's attention. However, I don't believe anything is a cold call—everything's a warm call if someone is breathing at the end of the phone. It's an uncommon point of view, but I love it! It's your job to make them feel warm and fuzzy about speaking to you on the phone, so you must have a good hook and opener. I usually include the same one-line openers over and over again. You must make sure you have their permission to get them on the phone and then have the time to position the problems you're solving. You must identify the problem and highlight the goal of the cold call, which is to remember that you have a solution that solves their problems. Therefore, the speed of identifying somebody's problem is essential. Once they're relaxed, your initial call should only take 15 minutes of their time because they didn't expect your call. It would help if you tried to get permission and time to spend more time with that individual, so they're willing to give you more time in their diary. And that's where you've got to demonstrate credibility, authenticity, trustworthiness and that you're an authority in your field. Someone that is seen as an expert. And if you can nail those five things within a minute or two, and you've got your elevator pitch, then you should be able to buy some time. You only need five minutes to uncover fundamental problems your product solves. Then it's asking for the next meeting. A lot of people make the mistake that they throw everything into the first call and don't realise the aim of the first call is to get a second call. The objective of the second call is to make a deep discovery then and demonstrate the product.

Although cold calling will never be as productive as warm calling, you shouldn't eliminate it from your sales strategy toolbox.

Try these six tried-and-true techniques for making successful cold calls.

Rather than listing all the features of your product, focus on how you can help the customer.

People aren't interested in what kinds of items you manufacture; instead, they care about how your products will improve their daily lives. If you can get that across, you've got a buyer. In other words, you shouldn't lead with "We make the best software on the market". Instead, say, "Our software offers excellent solutions to grow your business". Remember that it is value, not stuff, that consumers seek after. Provide a list of features and benefits only when customers request more information about your offering. To pique their interest, you should highlight how your solution would improve THEIR life rather than just that of their company. Tell them where to get more information on their own time if they need it before deciding to work with you or purchasing from you. While this approach to cold calling may not result in an immediate sale, it will create the path for a more fruitful follow-up contact, which is why it is so valuable.

Write a comprehensive script.

Feeling anxious is expected the first few times you make a cold call. If you're a novice sales professional who has never called a contact without first communicating with them via email or another method, this is extremely important to remember. Even some seasoned salespeople can feel that a cold call is scary. When you're anxious, you may talk too quickly, make mistakes, or forget what you are about to say. Avoid all these if you want to make cold calls in the sales industry. Your potential client may miss some points if you speak too quickly. In your panic, you're repeating yourself almost verbatim. Finally, if you remember essential topics, the prospect will only get the complete sales speech. Precisely what benefits would they receive from choosing your product or service? They only have part of the picture. Feeling scared is acceptable, especially if this is your first cold call or you're new to sales; however, you cannot be jumpy when talking with a prospect. A script to follow when making cold calls is helpful in this situation. This is a brilliant strategy for making cold calls. You can nail your sales pitch if you have a script outlining what to say, line by line. But don't let the fact that you're reading from a script make you sound robotic! You don't need to memorise the script, but you should use it as a reference. If you read the cold calling script, your prospect will recognise you as unnatural and dismiss you as uninterested. It's essential to maintain your upbeat, welcoming tone.

It's All Right to Make Small Talk

If someone picks up the phone, don't start talking right away! Despite common wisdom to the contrary, we've found that getting to know someone first leads to more significant results. Get to know the other person while talking about work-related topics. Make small talk by inquiring about their commute, how long it took them to get to work, or how their day is going. If you're trying to figure out if you're talking to the correct person or if they'd be interested in what you offer, this is a great method to find out.

Master the Appropriate Tone

Even if you use the perfect words to describe what you're selling, the sale will only go through if your tone of voice matches. Keep it from being monotonous. Speaking with assurance is also essential. A prospect's disinterest in doing business with you is directly proportional to your level of boredom. If you, the person selling the goods, can't muster enthusiasm, why should your potential customers? It isn't easy to sound confident and approachable on the phone every time, but it's essential. It would help if you exuded confidence and strength without appearing aggressive.

An excellent cold call strategy requires the complete absence of hostility. Yes, you want to book the meeting, but keep cool even when things aren't going your way.

Know When to Call

Nobody likes having to keep calling back the same potential customer. True, but only if you keep calling them at inappropriate hours. Friday afternoons are among the worst times to contact a potential client because most people have switched off from work. Monday mornings are also not ideal for creating a sales call, as it's common for people to be lethargic as they sluggishly make their way to work after the weekend. So how do you know when making a cold call is OK? Try Wednesday or Thursday. You never know when you might succeed, so find a routine that works for you.

Prepare thoroughly before making a cold call

Do your homework first before making that all-important first call. This is another one of the essential pointers for making cold calls. Research the likely decision-maker, the best time to reach them, and their function at the organisation. These specifics will determine the most effective strategy for generating buzz about your offering. Do the homework; don't just wing it. Skipping this process could result in you wasting time on the incorrect person. If you're uncomfortable asking "Who's in charge of......?" online, it may be time to contact a company contact for some insider knowledge. A simple LinkedIn search will reveal the name and contact information of the decision-maker at the company of the lead you were planning to call.

Prospecting

There are different prospecting avenues that you can take instead of the cold call. You can use prospect videos on LinkedIn or other sales technology stack tools. Email, depending on how you use it, is also an important prospecting tool. There are now sales tools out there, which I mentioned, the likes of SalesLoft and Outreach, which automatically follow up if someone hasn't responded in a specific time. You can send an email on day one; if someone hasn't replied, it can send an email to them three days later. You can send another email four days later if they still haven't responded. You should have an omnichannel approach, as they call it. So not only are you using email, but you should also be using the phone and leaving voicemails on people's phones. You should be sending them LinkedIn messages. There is also the option to try physical gifting where you send something in the post. This is thoughtful and highlights to the individual that you understand them; you know who their football team or rugby team is, for example. It's another way to get in front of them.

There's a program called ABM, which is called 'account-based marketing. It's a framework around identifying your key target ICP, which is your 'ideal customer profile'. From that, you need to build a strategy of touch points in your prospecting to get their attention. Ultimately, you're always trying to get their attention. The fundamental aim is to get them on the phone, but if they're not immediately picking up the phone, you then use email. You need to be on LinkedIn if they're not responding to your emails. Finally, there's a whole series of follow-ups. The key in all of this is the phrase 'follow up'. Nothing happens on that first call; sometimes, you're lucky and get through to the right person, but that's not the game. That's not why salespeople are paid as much as they are. More prospecting is required to get in front of someone across different channels.

While a sales lead has the potential to make an instant purchase, they are less likely to do so than a more qualified sales prospect. Once they have been qualified and moved up to the level of sales prospects, there is a much better chance that they will become paying customers.

Sales prospecting is easy to understand, but requires a lot of hard work. The process involves five stages, from first contact collection through final contract signing.

Make a Prospect List: The first step in sales prospecting is to make a list of possible customers. This can include both leads who have shown interest in your product and people you find through research. Include details like the names and contact information of potential customers, as well as details about their pain areas and level of interest in your product, if you have any.

As part of the sales process, it is essential to "qualify" prospects by learning as much as possible about them to determine if they are a good fit for further pursuit. To ensure you are contacting the proper person, you will need to research their job duties, the company's organisational structure, and their web presence.

The initial stages of a conversation consist of outreach and discovery calls. The goal of the outreach stage is to get potential customers interested in your product or service by talking to them directly over the phone. Then, there will be a separate meeting called the discovery call, where you will demonstrate your product or explore the prospect's needs and how your product might answer those needs.

Instruction on using a product can occur throughout several conference calls or in-person meetings. At this point, you will have taught the prospect all there is to know about your product and discovered their unique problems. During this phase, you'll also address any concerns the customer may have.

Previous Contacts

Potential customers may not have been interested in working with you at the time, but that may change. When contacting, don't forget to follow up on any previous possibilities.

According to LinkedIn research, nearly eighty per cent of salespeople have either no connections in their target accounts or only one person (single-threaded) connection. Only 7% of accounts were multi-threaded, meaning they were linked to six or more users. The sellers who use a multi-pronged strategy tend to have better results. There was an average increase of 34% in the win rate for new business-focused sellers when they used many threads instead of just one when approaching an account.

Connecting with people from previous opportunities and accounts is beneficial, as evidenced by the data. Potential customers may not have been interested in working with you at the time, but that may change. When contacting, don't forget to follow up on any previous possibilities.

What you're up against, usually, is people immediately trying to get you off the phone. They're objecting to you pitching them; they're objecting based on the fact that they don't understand what you do. Remember, you are the expert—they're not the expert. They are the expert in what they do, but they're not the expert in your technology and the problems that your technology solves. Common objections are:

- The time's not right.
- It sounds too expensive.
- I don't have the budget right now.
- How did you get my number?
- Why are you talking to me?
- I'm not the right person.

To overcome that objection of, "I'm not the right person", you must ask, "who is the right person in your business? Who is the person I can be talking to?"

Objection Handling

Objection handling is also a mindset, as it's undoubtedly one of the most frightening parts of sales. You are in a much better position to overcome objections around your product and pitch if you truly understand your product and the persona of the person you're targeting. This comes down to your competency and capability around your product and service offering. It takes a lot of practice, and that's why you need 'activity activity activity. It's simple—the more conversations you've had, the more objections you've handled, and the more rejections you've faced, the better you are at handling those objections.

Sales Process

Process is everything. From the first call discovery, the first meeting demo, then the proposal and then the close. Depending on what your product is, that process will be longer, depending on the sale's complexity. Much of the sales process now involves what they call 'a buying committee'. Many buyers are interested in deciding if your product is something the company should invest in overall. Therefore, the challenge is that it's not a linear or straightforward sales process. Although I would love it to be, you're often running multiple processes with multiple people within the organisation, which all need to match up. This means you have to connect people from your side of the organisation to theirs. For example, let's say you are dealing with someone technical; you need to find someone technically minded from your team who can connect with them on that level. Different parts of the platform or the product solve various problems for different people. Also, remember some people are more persuasive than others. You could be seen as a salesperson running your sales process, but you should be quarterbacking, coordinating, and orchestrating how you manage that process. Therefore, you need to bring in the right resources at each stage of that sales process. So, when you're at the demo stage, you might need a solutions engineer or a solutions consultant who can help you with the technical demonstration and answer any technical questions. And then there's proposal writing, ensuring that you're putting the right person in place to do that.

At each stage of the process, provide the client with value. The goal is to make sure that the stages of the sales process and the stages of the buyer's journey are in sync. In this manner, we can take care of the client's needs or problems whenever they arise. For instance, a point of sale with which we have attempted to get in touch and visited but were unsuccessful finds out all of a sudden that one of their suppliers is consistently making errors with the orders, raising costs, or making excessive demands about the display area.

This client is familiar with our business and our products and has interacted with our sales representative multiple times. Therefore, they are not strangers to us. Furthermore, they have agreed to do something through the bond we have established (devoting time to speak with us on the phone and meet with our representative). Therefore, this could be our chance to step in and offer a resolution to their issue. To assist in educating the sales team, provide guidelines with detailed instructions. The manager has a tried-and-true, clearly laid-out process that will enable them to achieve successful results, so they are not required to improvise. They don't need to spend many hours of trial and error trying to figure out what works or doesn't. They can also determine which phase a client is now in and what has to be done to move them on to the next one, such as initiating contact, setting up an appointment, presenting the quote, scheduling a second visit, placing an order, etc.

Last but not least, the business can identify and use specific training needs; for instance, if a salesperson stalls at one of the phases: they aren't generating any leads, they are scheduling very few visits, they are receiving very few orders, etc.

Predictability is increased through the application of a method. That is, there is no room for error when specific tasks are consistently carried out in the same manner by every team member. Furthermore, these predicted results are scalable by just increasing the actions undertaken.

Discovery

Discovery is all about asking questions early on in the process to identify qualification criteria. That means to identify the needs of the company, identify their pains and their problems, identify what their appetite is and if it's the right time to buy. There is a crossover between qualification and discovery, but it's important to call out discovery – it's such an important step of the process. If you haven't done an effective discovery, you don't know if you're going to be the right fit for that buyer or be the right product for that company. You need to make that decision, not them, because you're the one who has to decide if you're going to pursue it.

If there is genuinely a need in their business and you've done the right discovery, you'll be able to identify that you can help them in some way. And that's all you're trying to do as a salesperson; as much as trying to sell to close the deal, you can only sell and close the deal if you can actually help that individual and help them solve their problems.

Elite Sales People

The ambition for many people in the sales world is to be the top performer, and the top 10% is what I consider to be the elite. If you are the top performer in your organisation, you exhibit behaviours and habits that demonstrate that you understand how to run a sales process, run effective discovery, understand how to effectively qualify your activities smartly. It's your methodology, your approach, and the way you interact with other people in the business. It's how you apply yourself and you stand out. And that business is well regarded and well respected. If you apply everything in this book, you should be one of the elite and you should be standing out. Remember, it's how you behave as an individual that allows you to become an elite top performer.

Chapter Eleven
Selling Yourself

LinkedIn

WE ALL KNOW that LinkedIn is the most important online resource in sales, yet many people don't utilise the platform as much as they should. Here is a reminder why you should take LinkedIn more seriously and how to optimise your profile.

1. Establishing a Professional Presence: A well-crafted LinkedIn page can help establish a professional presence. It is an excellent platform to showcase your experience, skills, and accomplishments to potential employers, clients, and colleagues.

2. Building Connections: LinkedIn is an excellent platform for building connections with other sales professionals, potential customers, and business partners. You can use LinkedIn to find new leads, build relationships with prospects, and engage with their network.

3. Reputation Management: It can help manage a salesperson's reputation. A well-curated

profile that showcases your expertise, achievements, and values can enhance your professional reputation, making you more attractive to potential employers and customers.

4. Industry Insights: LinkedIn is a great platform for staying up-to-date with industry news and trends. You can use LinkedIn to follow industry thought leaders, participate in industry-related discussions, and stay informed about the latest developments in your field.

5. Job Opportunities: LinkedIn is a popular platform for recruiters and hiring managers. A well-crafted LinkedIn page can help you find new job opportunities and network with potential employers.

Overall, it's important for you to have a good LinkedIn page because it helps you build a professional presence, make connections, manage your reputation, stay up to date on your industry, and find new job opportunities.

How to optimise your LinkedIn profile

- Have a professional profile photo because it's your face that you are putting all over the internet and you should come across as an authority, as trustworthy, as likeable. There should be a smile.

- A strong headline that highlights the problem you're solving and what value you are adding to your audience. Rather than just using your job title, you could say, I solve X, Y, Z problem for X, Y, Z people.

- A good summary highlights the problems you're solving for companies and the solutions you're bringing to the table, as well as demonstrating your strengths and your story.

- Ensure you've got an explanation under your experience.

- Activate your network by making connection requests. The only way that your profile becomes useful is if you start connecting with people.

- Having conversations and opening with a hook that gets people interested in what you're doing. It's really important to have strong openers that allows a strong conversation starter, and then you can then go from there.

- You should be producing some form of content in your feed on a daily basis that is educating your audience about what you do and who you are. Every day I try to post some relevant content that's going to highlight to my audience that I am an expert and an authority in my field.

Personal Branding

Personal branding is about more than just creating a resume or having a fancy title. It's about creating a narrative that resonates with your audience and makes them remember you. It's about crafting stories and content that showcase your unique talents, experience, and personality.

Think of it this way: your personal brand is the statement that someone makes about you when you're not in the room. So what do people say about you? What do they know of you? What they see of you is what you put out on LinkedIn, so it's important to think carefully about the content you share.

To create a personal brand that stands out, you must demonstrate your authority, expertise, authenticity, enthusiasm, and even your sense of fun. These factors contribute to your personality and make you stand out from the crowd.

But how do you demonstrate these qualities? By producing content that showcases your unique perspective and talents. This could include articles, videos, infographics, or any other type of content that speaks to your target audience.

The key is ensuring your content is relevant to your target market and showcases your unique strengths. You want to hold their attention and create a narrative that builds trust and establishes you as an authority in your industry.

So, feel free to put yourself out there and create content that speaks to your target audience. With a solid personal brand, you'll become known for something in your industry and stand out from the competition.

Selling Over Zoom

The game has changed as a result of the pandemic and much more time is spent now online selling over

Zoom or whatever collaboration platform it might be, maybe Teams or Google Meet. With this new platform, there are some fundamentals that you need to take into consideration. You must remove all distractions from behind you (visually!) and make sure you've got a clear background. That, or you've got relevant props in the background that are conversation starters. So you might have some books that are important to you. You might have a picture or two that mean something, but overall you need to have a clean, professional background. I recommended that you set up your computer at eye line level. I've invested in the standup desk, which I highly recommend. I can adjust it up and down based on the requirement and get the right height and eye line alignment for a Zoom call so that it looks like I'm in the centre of the camera.

The underutilised Zoom trick is having a lighting ring. It means that your face is brightly lit and well rounded.

Then there is body language and facial expressions. As soon as someone turns on Zoom, you should have a beaming smile. You need to connect with people in the same way that you would do in person, and you can do that by looking directly into the camera and smiling so that's the first thing that greets them when they turn on the camera. Always maintain eye contact and turn off all distractions. That means making sure that your phone's turned off and making sure the doors are closed so you don't get distractions from pets or delivery people.

Then you've got to think about your body language again and how you are using your hands to emphasise points. It's important that hands can be seen on the screen and not hidden away so that they can emphasise points that you're making throughout the conversation.

Double check that the technology is working before you set off on your call that day. Make sure that your computer's fully up to speed with the latest upgrade, and that it's prepared to work in motion and in the right way so you are ready to perform when you need to. You don't want to get left short, which is then frustrating for the person at the receiving end.

This is basic, but *always* turns up on time. Many people excuse lateness due to 'back-to-back' calls, but I believe that you should be good at managing your time and finishing on schedule. Sometimes there are occasions when it's not possible, and there are things that happen, but in general you should do your best to be on time.

If you're in a group call, know who you are looking at. People tend to be more static and less animated on a call, and so it's more difficult to read the room. Reading the room is much easier in an in-person conversation in what I call the icebreaker moments or water cooler moments. That moment where someone says, "do you want a coffee or a tea?". On Zoom you tend to get straight down to business and it lacks that time for additional rapport building. Thus, you must make the extra effort with Zoom and add extra rapport building. This will help when you open that camera with a big beaming smile!

Board of Advisors

Companies have boards for a reason: to hold them to account and help them deliver the strategic objectives of a business. If you are savvy and working towards a strategic plan, you can create your own board of advisors and people in the industry that can help and advise you as you take on your goals and direction. We've discussed this earlier in the book, but make sure you have people there to guide you. A board of advisors is a group of people that don't necessarily have to come together as individuals. Still, they are individually aligned with your goals to help you achieve what you are setting out to achieve. In addition, there are mentors, someone I believe is many years ahead of you in their career, who acts as a guide to help you with your goals. This is different to a coach who is focused on holding you accountable.

A mentor gives up their time freely, is a few years ahead of you, is willing to support you and provides a sounding board. And then you have a coach or several coaches that you specifically pay to work on specific areas that you want to improve and develop. Coaches are an investment because they help you improve your game plan.

As I said earlier, I would use LinkedIn to find coaches and mentors. First, you can run searches to identify people in your industry with more experience than you. Then you need to send a personal message to say that you found their experience and profile interesting. Finally, ask them if they would be willing to support you in your career. The first connection is quite a light touch in that you should say you want to ask for some advice. Then, if you feel there's a connection, you can turn around and say, "look, I'm looking more deeply at having a mentor that can support me in my career".

Suppose they say yes, fantastic. And if they say no, you move on to the next person in your LinkedIn search.

At least with the mentoring, it should feel organic and more fluid when connecting. The coaching is more structured and specific. If you're paying for someone's time, you have a higher expectation of what they will deliver for you.

My psychologist is an important part of my advisor because she understands me deeply and what's impacting me. She gets what I'm trying to achieve. She knows me deeply and can provide guidance or a frame of reference based on what she's learned from me.

There are different types of individuals that you can bring into that board of advisors, but the important thing is they're specifically there for you. They should care about your development as an individual.

It can take a long time, but you can get therapy on the NHS. It is possible, but many companies have employee assistance programs, and as part of those employee systems programs, there's usually an allocation of hours to therapy. I would question the type of company if they do not have those support services in place because it should be the norm. There's a difference between being in crisis and in a desperate situation where you need that support immediately and between ongoing support from a maintenance perspective to maintain wellness or stability. My relationship with my therapist is to help me maintain that stability and maintain my well-being. It also acts as a preventative measure because, hopefully, she can catch changes in my mood, and I can catch them, too, by working together before they become too difficult to cope with.

Referrals

Referrals and recommendations are one of the best ways to be introduced to business. If you've truly delivered for a customer, then you can ask them for an introduction or a referral because that's going to tee you up and set up that meeting quicker than a cold outreach or prospecting message.

Remember to consider the importance of asking every person who has had a positive experience with you for a referral. Even if they haven't purchased from you, they will know someone in their network that could benefit from your service or offering. So ask for the referral, and then follow up over email or the phone, reminding the individual that they said they would make a referral. This is very important when generating additional business. And the more referrals you can generate, the more business you're going to generate and the easier it is to hit your numbers.

When asking for a referral, ask a question to understand if someone is satisfied with the interaction that they've had with you. If the answer is yes, then ask them why. Why did they enjoy it? Hopefully they'll give you an indication that you as an individual, played a part in making it a positive process. Then say, "as a result of that positive process, is it possible to get a recommendation, and could you pass on your details to a contact of theirs? Or would they be willing to introduce an email, via LinkedIn or over the phone to an individual who thinks they would also benefit from that interaction?"

Ask the question, understand why it's been a good experience, and then leverage that positive response to get that introduction teed up.

The New Buyer

If you used the example of a car purchase, you would go onto the forecourt or a dealership. You might visit multiple dealerships on that day, and the salesperson would have a chance to interact with you and influence the sales process. Because of the development of high-quality websites, that's all changed now. So much research is done from the individual's chair behind the computer researching different cars. So now you need to create a great digital experience, and you should be aware that when a buyer speaks to you, they might have as much knowledge as you do about the product. They've understood their problem and their needs, and they're already doing their research into that particular product.

The buyer is more informed than they've ever been. They can use reviews and comparison sites to pre-research your product before they speak to you. So, you've got to become an expert in your product, but you've also got to become an expert in your target industry, so you understand what your customers are facing. Then, you can converse professionally with them when they connect with you. Buyers today are much more informed than ever and have little patience for a long sales process—they want you to get straight to the point. That's why discovery is essential to balance asking questions, getting the information you wish to as a salesperson and presenting to the buyer what they want to see. They need to identify that what you are showing them solves their problem and is a practical and valuable contribution to their business.

One of the most difficult things for a new salesperson, especially in terms of confidence, is the new buyer. First, you have to learn about the buyer's perspective and their needs to build a solution based on your product or service.

Selling is a Team Sport

In particular, with technology, you've got a technology expert or what we call a solutions consultant or a solutions engineer. Somebody that is the technical expert on the software that you're selling.

Then you have someone making phone calls for you to book your meetings, which is known as a sales development representative. Alongside them, you'll have someone in customer success. Customer success is typically only available at post-sale. Still, a customer success manager who manages the relationship with the buyer once they've bought can influence that sales process. You've also got your manager aligning what we call multi-threading. That's aligning people from your business to the same level of people from the buyer's company. So if they've got a manager or a senior director that's going to be involved in the decision-making process, it's a good idea to align your senior director with theirs so that there is alignment. There's a positive touchpoint between both parties. And that goes the same with someone on the buyer side having a deeper understanding of the technology; you will want to align them with the solutions consultant.

Be grateful for the SDR that's brought to you the meeting because they've put in the effort into cold calling and making multiple phone calls to generate business for you as an individual. While they might not be at the front of the conversation, you've got to be grateful to the people who built the product in your company. Without that product, you don't have anything to sell. Thus, you can't hit your targets, and you don't have a job. So there are lots of individuals that are involved in allowing you to close a deal. And while you have the glory as an individual, you must thank others who support you during the sales process.

That is why sales is a team sport because there are multiple people involved in the sales process, and the more senior and the higher level business you're working in, the more critical it is to have that team in place.

Trying to do everything alone comes from naivety, ignorance, and a lack of experience. You might also miss opportunities because you're not aligning different people in your business with their businesses. Many salespeople struggle because they don't realise that they've got others in the team to lean on and contribute to their success.

A new salesperson might hesitate to speak to a manager because the manager is figuring out their suitability to continue in their company during their probation. Whereas actually, if you can engage your manager, that highlights to them that you are thinking about building value into your deals with other experts in the business. That allows you to demonstrate to your sales manager that you've got opportunities that deserve their input. There is often a lack of appreciation for the resources that you have around you as a salesperson, yet the more that you can leverage those resources, the people and the assets, the more successful you're going to be.

Conclusion

As I WRAP UP this book, I want to emphasise the importance of taking ownership over your mindset and well-being as a sales professional. Yes, hard skills are important, but your success and longevity in this career will ultimately depend on how you think and grow as a person. As someone who has experienced burnout firsthand, I can tell you that preventing it is much better than trying to cure it later.

I hope you have enjoyed the reminders and strategies to help you build a sustainable and enjoyable sales career. From practising gratitude to taking time out for yourself, implementing these concepts will allow you to ride the rollercoaster of sales with tremendous success and enjoyment.

And if you're interested in taking your sales career to the next level, I invite you to learn more about the Sales Confidence Membership. This program offers mentorship, coaching, peer groups, master classes, and networking opportunities to help you reach the next stage of your career. By taking this step, you'll be setting yourself apart and joining a community of high-growth individuals.

So, as you close this book and move forward in your sales career, remember to prioritise your mindset and personal development, and consider joining the Sales Confidence Membership to take your career to new heights.

As I reflect on the content of this book and the journey we've been on together, I'm reminded that knowledge alone isn't always enough. It's the implementation and accountability that truly propel us forward. I'm so excited to tell you about the Sales Confidence Membership, a program that gives you ongoing support and resources to help you reach your sales career goals.

Think of it as a powerful tool in your arsenal that keeps you on track and accountable throughout the year. It's designed to give you the best opportunity to become prosperous or even more successful than you already are. Whether you're just starting out or a seasoned sales veteran, Sales Confidence can help you get to that next level.

At Sales Confidence, our mission is to help you achieve your sales career aspirations. It could be landing your first sales job, becoming a manager, or even reaching the pinnacle of your sales career as a Chief Revenue Officer. Whatever your goal may be, we're here to support you every step of the way.

So as you put down this book and continue on your journey, I encourage you to consider the Sales Confidence Membership as your partner in success. With our help, you'll be on your way to achieving the sales career of your dreams.

Wishing you the best of luck until we meet again, (and I am confident we will!)

James Ski

The End

Website: https://www.salesconfidence.com

Phone: 07411973226

Email: james@salesconfidence.com

About The Author

JAMES SKI is the founder and CEO of Sales Confidence—the world's most valuable B2B sales community. Sales Confidence's mission is to help sales people and sales leaders at each stage of their career with their mindset, wellbeing, and performance.

Prior to setting up Sales Confidence, James was a director at LinkedIn, responsible for flagship enterprise accounts in the UK at one time the world's number 1 social seller, and has over ten years of experience building and leading sales teams. He advises companies on hiring, upskilling and scaling sales teams. Prior to LinkedIn, he helped the founding teams at Huddle, Ometria and Opogo grow sales.

James was born in Ascot, UK and grew up in the royal town of Windsor, UK. His early years were spent at The Windsor Boys' School, where he enjoyed playing rugby and competing in national rowing competitions. Following school, he pursued Business Innovation and Enterprise Studies at Oxford Brookes University and continued to row competitively.

James was taken to a mental health hospital while he was in university, and was diagnosed with bipolar disorder. Despite his diagnosis and the challenges of living with a mental illness, he has been able to develop a successful sales career and raise three wonderful children, Harry, Jack and Annabel.

This book is for anyone in business or sales who wants to learn how to gain Sales Confidence. While there are many fantastic books focused on sales tactics, Sales Confidence, teaches the mindset needed to build rock solid confidence and become extremely successful in sales.

Printed in Great Britain
by Amazon

48708472R00086